THE TRAGEDY OF TRAGEDIES

THE TRAGEDY OF TRAGEDIES

Henry Fielding

a *Broadview Anthology of British Literature* edition

Contributing Editor, *The Tragedy of Tragedies*:
Darryl P. Domingo, University of Memphis

General Editors,
Broadview Anthology of British Literature:
Joseph Black, University of Massachusetts, Amherst
Leonard Conolly, Trent University
Kate Flint, Rutgers University
Isobel Grundy, University of Alberta
Don LePan, Broadview Press
Roy Liuzza, University of Tennessee
Jerome J. McGann, University of Virginia
Anne Lake Prescott, Barnard College
Barry V. Qualls, Rutgers University
Claire Waters, University of California, Davis

broadview press

Library and Archives Canada Cataloguing in Publication

Fielding, Henry, 1707-1754
    Tragedy of tragedies / Henry Fielding ; contributing editor,
Darryl Domingo ; general editors, Joseph Black ... [et al.].
(Broadview anthology of British literature)
A play.
ISBN 978-1-55481-163-2

    I. Black, Joseph, 1962- II. Domingo, Darryl, 1978- III. Title.
IV. Series: Broadview anthology of British literature

PR3454.T6 2013   822'.5   C2012-907270-2

Broadview Press is an independent, international publishing house, incorporated in 1985.

We welcome comments and suggestions regarding any aspect of our publications—please feel free to contact us at the addresses below or at broadview@broadviewpress.com.

North America   PO Box 1243, Peterborough, Ontario, Canada K9J 7H5
                            2215 Kenmore Ave., Buffalo, New York, USA 14207
                            Tel: (705) 743-8990; Fax: (705) 743-8353
                            email: customerservice@broadviewpress.com

UK, Europe, Central Asia,   Eurospan Group, 3 Henrietta St., London WC2E 8LU, UK
Middle East, Africa, India, Tel: 44 (0) 1767 604972; Fax: 44 (0) 1767 601640
and Southeast Asia   email: eurospan@turpin-distribution.com

Australia and New Zealand NewSouth Books, c/o TL Distribution
                            15-23 Helles Ave., Moorebank, NSW, Australia 2170
                            Tel: (02) 8778 9999; Fax: (02) 8778 9944
                            email: orders@tldistribution.com.au

www.broadviewpress.com

Developmental Editors: Jennifer McCue and Laura Buzzard

Broadview Press acknowledges the financial support of the Government of Canada through the Canada Book Fund for our publishing activities.

This book is printed on paper containing 100% post-consumer fibre.

PRINTED IN CANADA

Contents

Introduction

Best known today as the father of the comic novel in English, Henry Fielding had a wide-ranging professional career that also included successful turns as a playwright, journalist, and Justice of the Peace for Middlesex and Westminster. Before even considering prose fiction, Fielding enjoyed a decade of fame as one of the most prodigious, innovative, and controversial playwrights of his day. At various points in his career, he contributed to and edited periodicals distinguished for their sharp political commentary and humorous reflections on the state of contemporary literature and culture. In his later life, his fairness and tough-on-crime attitude as the chief magistrate of London won him admiration from those who wished to combat the disorder and corruption of the city. Among his many achievements, Fielding helped to establish the "Bow Street Runners," a group that undertook raids to break up gangs of street robbers; it was an important precursor to the Metropolitan Police Service still operating in the London area today.

The oldest of seven children, Henry Fielding had a tumultuous childhood. His mother died a week before his eleventh birthday, and his father, a colonel who had expensive tastes and small means, lost custody of Henry and his siblings to their maternal grandmother after selling off much of their inheritance to pay his debts and finance an early remarriage. Given such a family situation, Fielding, despite being the eldest child and heir, was forced to make a living for himself.

Witty, passionate, and an excellent conversationalist with a strong sense of humor, the young Fielding chose playwriting as a promising career. London at the time boasted many playhouses and a large theatrical market; a talented playwright could do very well—and Fielding would become arguably the most popular playwright of the 1730s. After seeing his first play, *Love in Several Masques*, produced in 1728, Fielding left London temporarily to study in Holland at the University of Leiden. Upon his return, he staged four successful plays in one year (1730): *The Temple Beau, The Author's Farce, Tom Thumb*, and *Rape upon Rape: or, The Justice Caught in his Own Trap*. He went on to complete more than twenty-five plays in less than ten years, almost all of which were staged—an extraordinary output for an author still in his twenties through most of this period. While many critics, both in his own time and in later periods, found his work uneven, George Bernard Shaw (1856–1950) praised him as "the greatest dramatist, with the single exception of Shakespeare, produced in England between the Middle Ages and the nineteenth century." From 1732 to 1733, Fielding was the leading playwright of the Drury Lane Theatre, then the largest and most prestigious of London's theaters. In 1736 he took over management of the Little Theatre in the Haymarket, where he wrote plays for his own company of comedians.

A number of Fielding's plays were conventional five-act comedies in which he attempted to treat serious social themes, writing in the tradition of the master comedic playwrights he admired (such as Molière, William Congreve, George Farquhar, and William Wycherley); perhaps the most notable of these is *The Modern Husband* (1732). Far more successful, however, were his farces, ballad operas, and dramatic satires, which experimented with form, incorporated songs, and lambasted well-known personalities of the day. Among the most remarkable of these is *The Author's Farce*, Fielding's first smash hit, which satirized London's theatrical world by dramatizing the efforts of one Harry Luckless to become a successful dramatist. Luckless's puppet play, *The Pleasures of the Town*, is eventually staged—with actors performing the roles of the puppets—but success of this sort is uncertain and unstable; in the play's third and final act, the boundary between the world of the puppet play and the "real" world of *The Author's Farce* collapses, as Luckless is revealed to be related to his wooden characters.

Fielding also targeted government corruption and mismanagement, and at times he viciously criticized chief minister Sir Robert Walpole (although his political allegiances varied dramatically throughout his career). His *Grub Street Opera*, which mocked the royal family as well as both political parties, was notoriously withdrawn from the Haymarket Theatre before its opening night in 1731, likely because of political pressure. Fielding's playwriting career ended when the Stage Licensing Act of 1737 required that all plays be approved by a government examiner before they were produced, effectively censoring all theatrical work. It was widely suggested that the act was provoked in large part by the "seditious" content of Fielding's plays, and contemporaries claimed that the act was passed to silence one man. While that may be something of an exaggeration, there can be no doubt that he had touched a nerve.

Forced to make a career change, Fielding decided to pursue law, and in 1740 he was called to the bar. During the next few years he was plagued by financial trouble (and even briefly arrested for debt) as he built a career as a lawyer. He made money during this time by (anonymously) publishing satiric essays in anti-Walpole periodicals, establishing his own journal, and taking on several miscellaneous writing projects. One such project would change the direction of the rest of his career: *An Apology for the Life of Mrs. Shamela Andrews* (1741). This pamphlet-length parody of Samuel Richardson's first novel, *Pamela, or Virtue Rewarded* (1740), mocked its epistolary style and heavily moralistic tone. Though Fielding's little work was only one of many "anti-Pamelas" printed in the wake of *Pamela's* publication, his was particularly well received, and he was prompted to try his hand at comic prose fiction in a more earnest fashion. The result was *Joseph Andrews* (1742), supposedly a history of Pamela's virtuous brother Joseph, written, according to its title page, in imitation of Miguel de Cervantes, author of *Don Quixote*. Like Cervantes's work—and unlike *Pamela* and *Shamela*—*Joseph Andrews* is written as a sustained (albeit highly episodic) narrative rather than an extended exchange of letters. Fielding described the work in his preface as a "comic epic-poem in prose," a form he declared himself unable to "remember to have seen hitherto attempted in our language."

Fielding published his next novel, *Tom Jones* (1749), seven years after the success of *Joseph Andrews*. Readers embraced the book with such enthusiasm that at first the publisher struggled to keep up; the first print run sold out before its publication date, and three more editions—totaling a remarkable 10,000 copies—were printed before the end of the year. Considered Fielding's masterpiece, this picaresque novel details the hilarious episodes that lead to a foundling's coming into fortune. Yet the novel's most characteristic feature is its self-consciously chatty and intrusive narrator, who never misses an opportunity to digress on ethical quandaries or critical issues, and who never lets the reader forget who is telling the story. *Tom Jones* and *Joseph Andrews* together established the tradition of the comic novel in English.

Fielding completed one last novel, *Amelia* (1751), a story of a troubled marriage that contains elements of social protest. He also applied his wit to moral and literary commentary in the *Covent-Garden Journal* (1752), a new periodical that he sustained for almost a year while writing much of its content himself. However, much of his later life was taken up with his work as a magistrate. In 1753, in declining health as a result of cirrhosis of the liver, Fielding retired from public service. The following year he sailed to Portugal in the hopes of recovering his health. He died there, near Lisbon, where he was buried. His final journey is described with humor and pathos in *The Journal of a Voyage to Lisbon*, posthumously published in 1755.

The Tragedy of Tragedies: or, The Life and Death of Tom Thumb the Great

One of the greatest successes of Fielding's early playwriting career was *Tom Thumb*, a two-act play originally added as an afterpiece to *The Author's Farce*; when it was first performed in 1730, it ran to full houses for forty-one nights. Fielding began to revise the play during its initial run, and would eventually turn it into *The Tragedy of Tragedies*. With an added third act and the addition of the character of Glumdalca, *The Tragedy of Tragedies* is similar to the original *Tom Thumb* up to about halfway through the second act, but almost all the material past this point is new. In its revised and expanded version, the play is a parody of the heroic drama that has all the elements of the extravagant genre it mocks, including a superhuman hero (though of miniature size), a captive princess (of enormous size), a heroic battle (accompanied by thunder and lightning), and two (ridiculously convoluted) love triangles. By the time Fielding staged and published *The Tragedy of Tragedies*, heroic plays were no longer popular in the English theater—indeed, most of his specific targets are more than thirty years old. Fielding, however, revived the old-fashioned genre in order to direct his satire more generally at the misuses and abuses of language, exploiting the overwrought style of plays like John Dryden's *Aureng-Zebe* (1675) and John Banks's *The Albion Queens* (1704) to expose any writing that allows words to get in the way of meaning.

Heroic drama also facilitated Fielding's ridicule of false scholarship. *The Tragedy of Tragedies* was put forward as the work not of Henry Fielding, but of "H. Scriblerus Secundus," a pen name Fielding adopted for several of his plays, thereby placing himself in the tradition of Jonathan Swift, John Gay, and, especially, Alexander Pope, who founded the so-called Scriblerus Club in 1714 in an attempt to satirize "all false tastes in learning." Like the Scriblerians, Fielding attacks mindless pedantry and inflated writing, imitating the format of Pope's *Dunciad Variorum* (1729) in an ironic preface and in copious notes (written in the voice of Scriblerus for printed editions of the play) that treat *The Life and Death of Tom Thumb the Great* as a work of sublime genius, and which mock-learnedly identify more than forty plays whose best lines are ostensibly borrowed from the tragedy. The number of words in the annotations outnumber those in the playtext two to one, and Fielding's main joke is discovered in the disjunction between the play's silly plot and frivolous characters, and the extraordinary lengths to which Scriblerus Secundus goes to explain them.

The Tragedy of Tragedies first appeared on the stage in 1731. The play enjoyed five seasons of immense popularity and went on to inspire numerous adaptations. It even became a favorite choice for amateur domestic performances, particularly by and for children. Novelist Frances Burney recounts playing Huncamunca in one such performance, and Charles Dickens's son Henry played Tom Thumb in another.

A Note on the Text

In the original 1731 edition of *The Tragedy of Tragedies*, the commentary of H. Scriblerus Secundus appeared as lettered footnotes at the base of the printed page. So as to avoid confusion with modern editorial commentary, the lettered notes have been printed on the right pages of the present edition, parallel with the playtext appearing on the left. Numbered editor's notes appear at the base of the pages. The studied nature of the 1731 text suggests that Fielding was working and citing from printed editions of the more than forty plays parodied in *The Tragedy of Tragedies*. For this reason, the editorial notes assign each play a date of first publication, instead of a date of first performance.

❦❧❦

The Tragedy of Tragedies: or, The Life and Death of Tom Thumb the Great

H. Scriblerus Secundus, His Preface

The town hath seldom been more divided in its opinion than concerning the merit of the following scenes. Whilst some publicly affirmed that no author could produce so fine a piece but Mr. P——,[1] others have with as much vehemence insisted that no one could write anything so bad, but Mr. F——.[2]

Nor can we wonder at this dissention about its merit, when the learned world have not unanimously decided even the very nature of this tragedy. For though most of the universities in Europe have honoured it with the name of *egregium & maximi pretii opus, tragœdiis tam antiquis quam novis longe anteponendum*;[3] nay, Dr. B—— hath pronounced, *citiùs Maevii Æneadem quam Scribleri istius tragœdiam hanc crediderim, cujus autorem Senecam ipsum tradidisse haud dubitârim*;[4] and the great Professor Burman hath styled Tom Thumb, *heroum omnium tragicorum facilè principem*.[5] Nay, though it hath, among other languages, been translated into Dutch, and celebrated with great applause at Amsterdam (where burlesque[6] never came) by

---

1 *Mr. P——* Poet Alexander Pope (1688–1744), who adopted the ironic persona of "Martinus Scriblerus" for a number of his satires on dullness and false learning.

2 *Mr. F——* Henry Fielding.

3 *egregium ... anteponendum* Latin: a distinguished work of the greatest value, to be rated as by far the best tragedy, ancient or modern.

4 *Dr. B——* Classical scholar Dr. Richard Bentley (1662–1742), who was considered a tasteless pedant by Pope and Jonathan Swift, both of whom mocked him in their work; *citiùs ... dubitârim* Latin: "I would sooner have believed the *Aeneid* to be by Maevius than that this tragedy, which I would not hesitate to ascribe to Seneca himself, could be the work of one like Scriblerus." The *Aeneid* was written in the first century BCE by the Roman poet Virgil, whose famous epic was belittled by a second-rate critic named Maevius; Seneca the Younger was a first-century CE Roman philosopher and dramatist, best known for violent tragedies adapted from the Greek.

5 *Professor Burman* Dutch classical scholar Pieter Burmann (1688–1744), under whom Fielding studied from 1728 to 1729; *heroum ... principem* Latin: of all tragic heroes, easily the foremost.

6 *burlesque* Type of comedy in which distortion is used to evoke ridicule and laughter, either by treating a lofty subject in a trivial manner, or, as in Fielding's *Tragedy*, treating a low subject in an exaggerated manner.

the title of *Mynheer Vander Thumb*, the burgomasters[1] receiving it with that reverent and silent attention which becometh an audience at a deep tragedy. Notwithstanding all this, there have not been wanting[2] some who have represented these scenes in a ludicrous light; and Mr. D——[3] hath been heard to say, with some concern, that he wondered a tragical and Christian nation would permit a representation on its theatre so visibly designed to ridicule and extirpate everything that is great and solemn among us.

This learned critic and his followers were led into so great an error by that surreptitious and piratical copy which stole last year into the world;[4] with what injustice and prejudice to our author, I hope will be acknowledged by everyone who shall happily peruse this genuine and original copy. Nor can I help remarking, to the great praise of our author, that, however imperfect the former was, still did even that faint resemblance of the true *Tom Thumb* contain sufficient beauties to give it a run of upwards of forty nights, to the politest audiences. But, notwithstanding that applause which it received from all the best judges, it was as severely censured by some few bad ones, and, I believe, rather maliciously than ignorantly, reported to have been intended a burlesque on the loftiest parts of tragedy, and designed to banish what we generally call fine things from the stage.

Now, if I can set my country right in an affair of this importance, I shall lightly esteem any labour which it may cost. And this I the rather undertake, first, as it is indeed in some measure incumbent on me to vindicate myself from that surreptitious copy before mentioned, published by some ill-meaning people under my name. Secondly, as knowing myself more capable of doing justice to our author than any other man, as I have given myself more pains to arrive at a thorough understanding of this little piece, having for ten years together read nothing else; in which time, I think I may modestly presume, with the help of my English dictionary, to comprehend all the meanings of every word in it.

---

1 *burgomasters* Dutch.
2 *wanting* Lacking.
3 *Mr. D——* John Dennis (1657–1734), an irascible critic and playwright with whom Pope frequently quarrelled.
4 *that surreptitious ... world* Scriblerus Secundus is made to suggest that *Tom Thumb*, the original two-act play that Fielding published in 1730 (a second edition of which was published that same year under Scriblerus's name), was a pirated, inaccurate copy of *The Tragedy of Tragedies*.

But should any error of my pen awaken *Clariss.* Bentleium[1] to enlighten the world with his annotations on our author, I shall not think that the least reward or happiness arising to me from these my endeavours.

I shall waive at present, what hath caused such feuds in the learned world: whether this piece was originally written by Shakespeare,[2] though certainly that, were it true, must add a considerable share to its merit; especially with such who are so generous as to buy and to commend what they never read, from an implicit faith in the author only: a faith which our age abounds in as much as it can be called deficient in any other.

Let it suffice that the *Tragedy of Tragedies,* or, *The Life and Death of Tom Thumb,* was written in the reign of Queen Elizabeth.[3] Nor can the objection made by Mr. D——, that the tragedy must then have been antecedent to the history, have any weight, when we consider that though the *History of Tom Thumb,* printed by and for Edward M——r, at the Looking-Glass on London-Bridge,[4] be of a later date, still must we suppose this history to have been transcribed from some other, unless we suppose the writer thereof to be inspired: a gift very faintly contended for by the writers of our age. As to this history's not bearing the stamp of second, third, or fourth edition, I see but little in that objection, editions being very uncertain lights to judge of books by. And perhaps Mr. M——r may have joined twenty editions in one, as Mr. C——l[5] hath ere now divided one into twenty.

Nor doth the other argument, drawn from the little care our author hath taken to keep up to the letter of the history, carry any

---

1 *Clariss. Bentleium* Abbreviation for the Latin *clarissimum,* meaning "most illustrious" Bentley, a mocking imitation of learned forms of address.
2 *Shakespeare* During the early part of the eighteenth century, William Shakespeare (1564–1616) was particularly well known for his tragedies, which were performed regularly at the patent theaters.
3 *the reign of Queen Elizabeth* Elizabeth I reigned from 1558 to 1603. By dating *The Life and Death of Tom Thumb* to the Elizabethan period, and having Scriblerus Secundus claim that works published as early as 1613 and as late as 1731 borrowed from the tragedy, Fielding pokes fun at bad historical scholarship.
4 *Edward ... Bridge* Edward Midwinter was a publisher of cheap, popular print works. The location of his shop on London Bridge was a highly undesirable one.
5 *Mr. C—l* Edmund Curll (1675–1747), an unscrupulous publisher and antagonist of Pope, who notoriously multiplied "new" editions of a work by replacing the title page of the first edition with a fresh one. Scriblerus Secundus suggests that Edward Midwinter could have done the opposite by collapsing several editions into one.

greater force. Are there not instances of plays wherein the history is so perverted that we can know the heroes whom they celebrate by no other marks than their names? Nay, do we not find the same character placed by different poets in such different lights that we can discover not the least sameness, or even likeness in the features? The Sophonisba of Mairet, and of Lee, is a tender, passionate, amorous mistress of Massinissa; Corneille and Mr. Thomson give her no other passion but the love of her country, and make her as cool in her affection to Massinissa, as to Syphax.[1] In the two latter, she resembles the character of Queen Elizabeth; in the two former she is the picture of Mary, Queen of Scotland.[2] In short, the one Sophonisba is as different from the other as the Brutus of Voltaire is from the Marius Jun. of Otway; or as the Minerva is from the Venus[3] of the ancients.

Let us now proceed to a regular examination of the tragedy before us, in which I shall treat separately of the fable, the moral, the characters, the sentiments, and the diction.[4]

And first of the fable, which I take to be the most simple imaginable; and, to use the words of an eminent author, "One, regular and uniform, not charged with a multiplicity of incidents, and yet affording several revolutions of fortune; by which the passions may be excited, varied, and driven to their full tumult of emotion."[5] Nor is

---

1 *The Sophonisba ... Syphax* Sophonisba was a Carthaginian noblewoman married to Syphax, King of Numidia, who was defeated by Massinissa, a Numidian prince in alliance with Rome, in 203 BCE. Massinissa subsequently fell in love with Sophonisba, but rather than see her return to Rome a captive, he convinced her to kill herself by drinking poison. This story was the subject of numerous plays and operas, several of which Scriblerus Secundus references here: Jean Mairet's *Sophonisbe* (1634), Nathaniel Lee's *Sophonisba* (1676), Pierre Corneille's *Sophonisbe* (1663), and James Thomson's *The Tragedy of Sophonisba* (1730), which the notes usually identify as the "new" *Sophonisba*.

2 *Mary, Queen of Scotland* Queen Mary I of Scotland was forced to abdicate the Scottish throne in 1567, and was later executed as a traitor for attempting to assassinate Queen Elizabeth of England, whose kingdom she sought to inherit.

3 *Brutus of ... Otway* Brutus and Marius Junior each appear in a different play set in Augustan Rome: *Brutus* (1730) by François Voltaire and *The History and Fall of Caius Marius* (1680) by Thomas Otway, respectively; *Minerva ... Venus* Minerva and Venus were Roman goddesses; Minerva was associated with wisdom and war, and Venus with love and beauty.

4 *Let us now ... and the diction* In his preliminary commentary on *The Dunciad Variorum* (1729), Martinus Scriblerus examines Pope's mock-epic poem under similar heads. Both Pope and Fielding parody the stiff formalism of French neoclassical critics like René Rapin (1621–87) and René Le Bossu (1631–80), and of English exponents like Dennis.

5 *One, regular ... emotion* From the preface to Thomson's *Sophonisba*, mentioned above.

the action of this tragedy less great than uniform. The spring of all is the love of Tom Thumb for Huncamunca; which causeth the quarrel between their Majesties in the first act; the passion of Lord Grizzle in the second; the rebellion, fall of Lord Grizzle and Glumdalca, devouring of Tom Thumb by the cow, and that bloody catastrophe in the third.

Nor is the moral of this excellent tragedy less noble than the fable; it teaches these two instructive lessons, *viz.*[1] that human happiness is exceeding transient, and that death is the certain end of all men; the former whereof is inculcated by the fatal end of Tom Thumb; the latter, by that of all the other personages.

The characters are, I think, sufficiently described in the *Dramatis Personae*; and I believe we shall find few plays where greater care is taken to maintain them throughout, and to preserve in every speech that characteristical mark which distinguishes them from each other. "But (says Mr. D——) how well doth the character of Tom Thumb, whom we must call the hero of this tragedy, if it hath any hero, agree with the precepts of Aristotle, who defineth tragedy to be the imitation of a short but perfect action, containing a just greatness in itself, etc.[2] What greatness can be in a fellow whom history relateth to have been no higher than a span?"[3] This gentleman seemeth to think, with Sergeant Kite,[4] that the greatness of a man's soul is in proportion to that of his body, the contrary of which is affirmed by our English physognominical writers. Besides, if I understand Aristotle right, he speaketh only of the greatness of the action, and not of the person.

As for the sentiments and the diction, which now only remain to be spoken to; I thought I could afford them no stronger justification than by producing parallel passages out of the best of our English writers. Whether this sameness of thought and expression which I have quoted from them proceeded from an agreement in their way of thinking, or whether they have borrowed from our author, I leave the reader to determine. I shall adventure to affirm this of the sentiments

---

1   *viz.* Short for the Latin *videlicet*, meaning "that is to say," or "namely."
2   *Aristotle ... itself, etc.* Dennis's reference is to Aristotle's *Poetics* (1449b).
3   *span* The distance from the tip of the thumb to that of the little finger.
4   *Sergeant Kite* A character in George Farquhar's 1706 comedy, *The Recruiting Office*. In an attempt to attract new recruits, Kite contends in the first scene of the play that "he that has the good fortune to be born six foot high, was born to be a great man."

of our author; that they are generally the most familiar which I have ever met with, and at the same time delivered with the highest dignity of phrase; which brings me to speak of his diction. Here I shall only beg one postulatum,[1] *viz.* that the greatest perfection of the language of a tragedy is that it is not to be understood; which granted (as I think it must be), it will necessarily follow that the only way to avoid this is by being too high or too low for the understanding, which will comprehend everything within its reach. Those two extremities of style Mr. Dryden illustrates by the familiar image of two inns,[2] which I shall term the aerial and the subterrestrial.

Horace goeth farther, and showeth when it is proper to call at one of these inns, and when at the other:

> *Telephus & Peleus, cùm pauper & exul uterque,*
> *Projicit ampullas & sesquipedalia verba.*[3]

That he approveth of the *sesquipedalia verba* is plain; for had not *Telephus & Peleus* used this sort of diction in prosperity, they could not have dropped it in adversity. The aerial inn, therefore (says Horace) is proper only to be frequented by princes and other great men, in the highest affluence of fortune; the subterrestrial is appointed for the entertainment of the poorer sort of people only, whom Horace advises,

> ——*dolere sermone pedestri.*[4]

The true meaning of both which citations is that bombast is the proper language for joy, and doggerel[5] for grief, the latter of which is

---

1 *postulatum* Fundamental principle.
2 *Mr. Dryden ... two inns* In his essay "Of Heroic Plays" (1672), poet, playwright, and critic John Dryden (1631–1700) argues against those who recognize that serious plays should transcend the prose of ordinary conversation, but who do not admit that rhyming poetry is best for the stage; such people, he says, are lodging themselves "in the open field between two inns," because they "have lost that which [they] call natural, and have not required the last perfection of art."
3 *Telephus ... verba* Latin: "Both Telephus and Peleus, as paupers and in exile, abandoned bombast and six-foot long words." From the *Ars Poetica* of the first-century BCE Roman poet Horace.
4 *dolere ... pedestri* Latin: "grieve in ordinary prose." Again, from the *Ars Poetica*.
5 *bombast* Inflated language used to describe a commonplace subject; *doggerel* Irregular or badly composed comic verse.

literally implied in the *sermo pedestris*, as the former is in the *sesqui-pedalia verba*.

Cicero recommendeth the former of these: *quid est tam furiosum vel tragicum quàm verborum sonitus inanis, nullâ subjectâ sententiâ neque scientiâ.*[1] What can be so proper for tragedy as a set of big sounding words, so contrived together as to convey no meaning; which I shall one day or other prove to be the sublime of Longinus.[2] Ovid declareth absolutely for the latter inn:

> *Omne genus scripti gravitate tragaedia vincit.*[3]

Tragedy hath of all writings the greatest share in the *bathos*,[4] which is the profound of Scriblerus.[5]

I shall not presume to determine which of these two styles be properer for tragedy. It sufficeth that our author excelleth in both. He is very rarely within sight through the whole play, either rising higher than the eye of your understanding can soar, or sinking lower than it careth to stoop. But here it may perhaps be observed that I have given more frequent instances of authors who have imitated him in the sublime than in the contrary. To which I answer, first, bombast being properly a redundancy of genius, instances of nature occur in poets whose names do more honour to our author than the writers in the doggerel, which proceeds from a cool, calm, weighty way of thinking. Instances whereof are most frequently to be found in authors of a lower class. Secondly, that the works of such authors are difficultly found at all. Thirdly, that it is a very hard task to read them, in order

---

1 *quid est ... scientiâ* A very loose paraphrase of first-century BCE Roman orator Cicero's *De Oratore* (*On the Orator*). The original translates as: "for what savors so much of madness as the empty sound of words, even the choicest and most eloquent, when there is no sense or knowledge contained in them?" Scriblerus Secundus provides a translation of his misquotation, which inverts the meaning of the original.

2 *Longinus* Third-century CE Greek rhetorician who is conventionally ascribed authorship of *On the Sublime*, a treatise that argues that good writing is that which achieves "elevation," rising above the ordinary in both style and subject.

3 *Omne ... vincit* Latin: "Tragedy surpasses all other kinds of writing in the matter of seriousness." From first-century BCE Roman poet Ovid's *Tristia* (*Sorrows*).

4 *bathos* Unintentional.

5 *Scriblerus* Martinus Scriblerus, the "author" of Pope's *Peri Bathous; or, The Art of Sinking in Poetry* (1728). The following paragraph echoes that treatise's humorous defense of the *bathos* as the opposite extreme of the sublime.

to extract these flowers from them. And lastly, it is very often difficult to transplant them at all; they being like some flowers of a very nice nature, which will flourish in no soil but their own: For it is easy to transcribe a thought, but not the want of one. *The Earl of Essex*,[1] for instance, is a little garden of choice rarities, whence you can scarce transplant one line so as to preserve its original beauty. This must account to the reader for his missing the names of several of his acquaintance, which he had certainly found here, had I ever read their works; for which, if I have not a just esteem, I can at least say with Cicero, *quae non contemno, quippè quae nunquam legerim*.[2] However, that the reader may meet with due satisfaction in this point, I have a young commentator from the university who is reading over all the modern tragedies at five shillings a dozen, and collecting all that they have stole from our author, which shall shortly be added as an appendix to this work.

DRAMATIS PERSONAE

MEN

King Arthur, *a passionate sort of king, husband to Queen Dollalolla, of whom he stands a little in fear; father to Huncamunca, whom he is very fond of; and in love with Glumdalca.*

Tom Thumb the Great, *a little hero with a great soul, something violent in his temper, which is a little abated by his love for Huncamunca.*

Ghost of Gaffer[3] Thumb, *a whimsical sort of ghost.*

Lord Grizzle, *extremely zealous for the liberty of the subject,[4] very choleric[5] in his temper, and in love with Huncamunca.*

---

1 *The Earl of Essex The Unhappy Favourite: Or the Earl of Essex* (1682), by John Banks, who was known for the dramatic sentimentality—but not necessarily the good quality—of his plays.

2 *quae ... legerim* Latin: "those that I do not despise, because I have never read them." From *Tusculan Disputations*, where Cicero speaks of books by would-be philosophers.

3 *Gaffer* Title of respect given to elderly men, similar to "Master," but indicating a lower rank.

4 *zealous for ... the subject* Passionate about individual liberties.

5 *choleric* Hot-tempered.

Merlin, *a conjurer, and in some sort father to Tom Thumb.*
Noodle *and* Doodle, *courtiers in place,*[1] *and consequently of that party that is uppermost.*
Foodle, *a courtier that is out of place, and consequently of that party that is undermost.*
Bailiff *and* Follower, *of the party of the plaintiff.*
Parson, *of the side of the church.*

WOMEN

Queen Dollalolla, *wife to King Arthur, and mother to Huncamunca, a woman entirely faultless, saving that she is a little given to drink, a little too much a virago*[2] *towards her husband, and in love with Tom Thumb.*
The Princess Huncamunca, *daughter to their Majesties King Arthur and Queen Dollalolla, of a very sweet, gentle, and amorous disposition, equally in love with Lord Grizzle and Tom Thumb, and desirous to be married to them both.*
Glumdalca, *of the giants, a captive Queen, beloved by the King, but in love with Tom Thumb.*
Cleora, *maid of honour, in love with Noodle.*
Mustacha, *maid of honour, in love with Doodle.*

Courtiers, Guards, Rebels, Drums, Trumpets, Thunder and Lightning.

Scene: *The court of King Arthur, and a plain thereabouts.*

---

1   *courtiers in place* Court attendants in government.
2   *virago* Overbearing, quarrelsome woman.

ACT 1, Scene 1. The Palace.

(*Doodle, Noodle.*)

DOODLE. Sure, such a [a] day as this was never seen!
    The sun himself, on this auspicious day,
    Shines, like a beau in a new birthday suit:
    This down the seams embroidered, that the beams.
    All nature wears one universal grin.
NOODLE. This day, O Mr. Doodle, is a day
5   Indeed, [b] a day we never saw before.

a Corneille[1] recommends some very remarkable day, wherein to fix the action of a tragedy. This the best of our tragical writers have understood to mean a day remarkable for the serenity of the sky, or what we generally call a fine summer's day: so that according to this their exposition, the same months are proper for tragedy, which are proper for pastoral. Most of our celebrated English tragedies, as *Cato, Mariamne, Tamerlane,* &c. begin with their observations on the morning. Lee seems to have come the nearest to this beautiful description of our author's:

> The morning dawns with an unwonted crimson,
> The flowers all odorous seem, the garden birds
> Sing louder, and the laughing sun ascends
> The gaudy earth with an unusual brightness,
> All nature smiles.   *Caes. Borg.*

Massinissa in the new *Sophonisba* is also a favourite of the sun:

> ————————————The sun too seems
> As conscious of my joy with broader eye
> To look abroad the world, and all things smile
> Like Sophonisba.

Memnon in the *Persian Princess*[2] makes the sun decline rising, that he may not peep on objects, which would profane his brightness.

> ————————————The morning rises slow,
> And all those ruddy streaks that used to paint
> The day's approach are lost in clouds as if
> The horrors of the night had sent 'em back
> To warn the sun he should not leave the sea,
> To peep, &c.

b This line is highly conformable to the beautiful simplicity of the ancients. It hath been copied by almost every modern·[3]

> Not to be is not to be in woe.   *State of Innocence.*
> Love is not sin but where 'tis sinful love.   *Don Sebastian.*
> Nature is nature, Laelius.   *Sophonisba.*
> Men are but men, we did not make ourselves.   *Revenge.*

---

1   *Corneille* Innovative French tragedian and critic, Pierre Corneille (1606–84), in his *Discours des trios unites* (1660).
2   *celebrated English tragedies* Scriblerus Secundus alludes to Joseph Addison's *Cato* (1713), Elijah Fenton's *Mariamne* (1723), and Nicholas Rowe's *Tamerlane* (1702), and quotes lines from Lee's *Caesar Borgia* (1680), Thomson's *The Tragedy of Sophonisba* (1730), and Lewis Theobald's *The Persian Princess* (1715).
3   *every modern* The lines are "copied by" (i.e., parodies of) Dryden's *The State.*

The mighty ^c Thomas Thumb victorious comes;
Millions of giants crowd his chariot wheels,
10   ^d Giants! to whom the giants in Guildhall¹
Are infant dwarfs. They frown, and foam, and roar,
While Thumb regardless of their noise rides on.
So some cock-sparrow° in a farmer's yard,   *male sparrow*
Hops at the head of an huge flock of turkeys.
15 DOODLE. When Goody² Thumb first brought this Thomas forth,
The genius of our land triumphant reigned;
Then, then, oh Arthur! did thy genius reign.

---

1   *Guildhall* The seat of government in London, where two carved giants, Gog and
Magog, sit on pedestals.
2   *Goody* I.e., Mrs.

^c Dr. B——y reads "the mighty Tall-mast Thumb." Mr. D——s "the mighty Thumping Thumb." Mr. T——d reads "Thundering." I think "Thomas" more agreeable to the great simplicity so apparent in our author.[1]

^d That learned historian Mr. S——n in the third number of his criticism on our author, takes great pains to explode this passage. "It is," says he, "difficult to guess what giants are here meant, unless the Giant Despair in the *Pilgrim's Progress*, or the Giant Greatness in *The Royal Villain*; for I have heard of no other sort of giants in the reign of King Arthur."[2] Petrus Burmanus makes three Tom Thumbs, one whereof he supposes to have been the same person whom the Greeks called Hercules, and that by these giants are to be understood the centaurs slain by that hero. Another Tom Thumb he contends to have been no other than the Hermes Trismegistus of the ancients. The third Tom Thumb he places under the reign of King Arthur, to which third Tom Thumb, says he, the actions of the other two were attributed. Now though I know that this opinion is supported by an assertion of Justus Lipsius, "*Thomam illum Thumbum non alium quam Herculem fuisse satis constat*";[3] yet shall I venture to oppose one line of Mr. Midwinter against them all:

In Arthur's court Tom Thumb did live.[4]

But then, says Dr. B——y, if we place Tom Thumb in the court of King Arthur, it will be proper to place that court out of Britain, where no giants were ever heard of. Spenser, in his *Fairy Queen*, is of another opinion, where describing Albion he says,

——Far within a salvage nation dwelt

Of hideous giants.

And in the same canto,

(continued)

---

1   *Dr. B——y* Bentley; *reads* Asserts that the correct text says (with the implication that the present text is flawed); *Mr. D——s* Dennis; *Mr. T——d* Theobald. The note ridicules critics who "over-read" texts, straining to explain them in the most artful way possible.

2   *Mr. S——n* Nathaniel Salmon (1675–1742), antiquarian and critic; *Giant Despair* Character in John Bunyan's 1678 religious allegory; *Giant Greatness* Referring to the line "swell this unknown ill to giant greatness" in Theobald's *Persian Princess*, subtitled *The Royal Villain*.

3   *Petrus Burmanus* Pieter Burmann; *Hermes Trismegistus* "Thrice-Great Hermes," a divine author to whom a collection of alchemical texts were attributed; *Justus Lipsius* Joose Lips (1547–1606), Belgian philologist; *Thomam ... constat* Latin: "Thomas Thumb, who it is agreed was none other than Hercules."

4   *Mr. Midwinter* Quotation from a lost chapbook edition of *The Famous History of Tom Thumb*, published by Midwinter.

NOODLE. They tell me it is [e] whispered in the books
Of all our sages that this mighty hero,
20 By Merlin's art° begot, hath not a bone   *sorcery*
Within his skin, but is a lump of gristle.
DOODLE. Then 'tis a gristle of no mortal kind,
Some God, my Noodle, stepped into the place
Of Gaffer Thumb, and more than [f] half begot
25 This mighty Tom.
NOODLE. [g]   Sure he was sent express
From Heav'n, to be the pillar of our state.
Though small his body be, so very small,
A chairman's leg is more than twice as large;
30 Yet is his soul like any mountain big,
And as a mountain once brought forth a mouse,
[h] So doth this mouse contain a mighty mountain.

Then Elfar, who two brethren giants had,
The one of which had two Heads———
    The other three.[1]
Risum teneatis, Amici.[2]

e To whisper in books, says Mr. D———s, is errant nonsense. I am afraid this learned man does not sufficiently understand the extensive meaning of the word "whisper." If he had rightly understood what is meant by the "senses whisp'ring the soul" in *The Persian Princess*, or what "whisp'ring like winds" is in *Aureng-Zebe*, or "like thunder" in another author, he would have understood this. Emmeline in Dryden sees a voice, but she was born blind, which is an excuse Panthea cannot plead in *Cyrus*, who hears a sight:

———Your description will surpass
All fiction, painting, or dumb show of horror,
That ever ears yet heard, or eyes beheld.

When Mr. D———s understands these he will understand whisp'ring in books.[3]

f   —Some ruffian stepped into his father's place,
And more than half begot him.   *Mary Q. of Scots.*[4]

g   —— For Ulamar seems sent express from heaven,
To civilize this rugged Indian clime.   *Liberty Asserted.*[5]

h "*Omne majus continet in se minus, sed minus non in se majus continere potest*," says Scaliger in *Thumbo*,[6]—I suppose he would have cavilled at these beautiful lines in *The Earl of Essex*:

Thy most inveterate soul,
That looks through the foul prison of thy body.

And at those of Dryden,

The palace is without too well designed,
Conduct me in, for I will view thy mind.   *Aureng Zebe.*

---

1   *Spenser* From *The Faerie Queene* (1590–96), Book II Canto X.
2   *Risum ... Amici* Latin: "Restrain your laughter, friends," from Horace's *Ars Poetica.*
3   *senses whisp'ring* Theobald, *The Persian Princess*; *whisp'ring like winds* Dryden, *Aureng-Zebe* (1675); *like thunder* Perhaps Benjamin Martyn, *Timoleon* (1730). Emmeline appears in Dryden's *King Arthur: or, The British Worthy* (1691), and Panthea in Banks's *Cyrus the Great: or, The Tragedy of Love* (1696).
4   *Mary Q. of Scots* Banks, *The Albion Queens: or, The Death of Mary Queen of Scotland* (1704).
5   *Liberty Asserted* By Dennis (1704).
6   *Omne ... potest* Latin: "The greater contains the lesser, but the lesser does not contain the greater"; *Scaliger* Julius Caesar Scaliger (1484–1558), French classicist regularly cited during this period for his commentaries on ancient literary texts. *Thumbo* and the quoted lines are of Fielding's invention.

DOODLE. Mountain indeed! So terrible his name,
[i] The giant nurses frighten children with it;
35   And cry "Tom Thumb is come, and if you are
Naughty, will surely take the child away."
NOODLE. But hark! [j] these trumpets speak the King's approach.
DOODLE. He comes most luckily for my petition.

(*Flourish.*)

ACT I, SCENE 2

(*King, Queen, Grizzle, Noodle, Doodle, Foodle.*)

KING. [k] Let nothing but a face of joy appear;
The man who frowns this day shall lose his head,
That he may have no face to frown withal.
Smile, Dollalolla—Ha! what wrinkled sorrow,
5   [l] Hangs, sits, lies, frowns upon thy knitted brow?
Whence flow those tears fast down thy blubbered cheeks,
Like a swollen gutter, gushing through the streets?
QUEEN. [m] Excess of joy, my Lord, I've heard folks say,
Gives tears as certain as excess of grief.
10   KING. If it be so, let all men cry for joy,
[n] 'Till my whole court be drowned with their tears;
Nay, till they overflow my utmost land,
And leave me nothing but the sea to rule.
DOODLE. My Liege, I a petition have here got.
15   KING. Petition me no petitions, sir, today;
Let other hours be set apart for business.

i Mr. Banks hath copied this almost verbatim:
It was enough to say, here's Essex come,
And nurses stilled their children with the fright. *E. of Essex.*

j The trumpet in a tragedy is generally as much as to say enter King: which makes Mr. Banks in one of his plays[1] call it "the trumpet's formal sound."

k Phraortes in *The Captives*[2] seems to have been acquainted with King Arthur.
Proclaim a festival for seven days' space,
Let the court shine in all its pomp and lustre,
Let all our streets resound with shouts of joy;
Let music's care-dispelling voice be heard,
The sumptuous banquet, and the flowing goblet
Shall warm the cheek, and fill the heart with gladness.
Astarbe shall sit mistress of the feast.

l Repentance frowns on thy contracted brow. *Sophonisba.*
Hung on his clouded brow, I marked despair. *Ibid.*
————A sullen gloom
Scowls on his brow. *Busiris.*[3]

m Plato is of this opinion, and so is Mr. Banks;
Behold these tears sprung from fresh pain and joy. *E. of Essex.*

n These floods are very frequent in the tragic authors.
Near to some murmuring brook I'll lay me down,
Whose waters if they should too shallow flow,
My tears shall swell them up till I will drown. *Lee's Sophonisba.*
Pouring forth tears at such a lavish rate,
That were the world on fire, they might have drowned
The wrath of heav'n, and quenched the mighty ruin *Mithridates.*[4]
One Author changes the Waters of Grief to those of Joy,
————These Tears that sprung from Tides of Grief
Are now augmented to a Flood of Joy. *Cyrus the Great.*
Another
Turns all the streams of hate, and makes them flow
In pity's channel. *Royal Villain.*

(continued)

---

1   *in one of his plays* Banks, *Cyrus the Great.*
2   *The Captives* By John Gay (1724).
3   *Busiris* By Edward Young (1719).
4   *Mithridates* Lee, *Mithridates, King of Pontus* (1678).

Today it is our pleasure to be ° drunk,
20   And this our Queen shall be as drunk as We.
QUEEN. (Though I already ᴾ half seas over am)
        If the capacious goblet overflow
        With arrack-punch¹ —'fore George!² I'll see it out;
        Of rum and brandy, I'll not taste a drop.
25   KING. Though rack,° in punch, eight shillings be a quart,   *arrack*
        And rum and brandy be no more than six,
        Rather than quarrel, you shall have your will.

(*Trumpets.*)

But, ha! the warrior comes; the great Tom Thumb;
The little hero, giant-killing boy,
Preserver of my kingdom, is arrived.

ACT I, SCENE 3

(*Tom Thumb, to them with Officers, Prisoners, and Attendants.*)

KING. �۹ Oh! welcome most, most welcome to my arms.
        What gratitude can thank away the debt
5   Your valour lays upon me?
QUEEN. (*Aside.*) ʳ   Oh! ye Gods!
TOM THUMB. When I'm not thanked at all, I'm thanked enough,
        ˢ I've done my duty, and I've done no more.
QUEEN. (*Aside.*) Was ever such a Godlike creature seen!

---

1   *arrack-punch* Sweet flavored liquor.
2   *'fore George* An oath, like "by George!", referring to St. George, the patron saint of England.

One drowns himself:

 ——Pity like a torrent pours me down,
  Now I am drowning all within a deluge.   *Anna Bullen*.[1]
Cyrus drowns the whole world:
  Our swelling grief [...]
  Shall melt into a deluge, and the world
  Shall drown in tears.   *Cyrus the Great*.

[o] An expression vastly beneath the dignity of tragedy, says Mr. D——s, yet we find the word he cavils at in the mouth of Mithridates less properly used and applied to a more terrible idea;
  I would be drunk with death.   *Mithrid*.
The author of the new *Sophonisba* taketh hold of this monosyllable, and uses it pretty much to the same purpose,
  The Carthaginian sword with Roman blood
  Was drunk.
I would ask Mr. D——s which gives him the best idea, a drunken King, or a drunken sword?
Mr. Tate dresses up King Arthur's resolution in heroics,
  Merry, my Lord, o'th'Captain's humour right,
  I am resolved to be dead drunk tonight.
Lee also uses this charming Word;
  Love's the drunkenness of the mind.   *Gloriana*.[2]

[p] Dryden hath borrowed this, and applied it improperly:
  I'm half seas o'er in death.   *Cleom*.[3]

[q] This figure is in great use among the tragedians;
  'Tis therefore, therefore 'tis.   *Victim*.[4]
  I long repent, repent and long again.   *Busiris*.

[r] A tragical exclamation.

[s] This Line is copied verbatim in *The Captives*.

---

1 *Anna Bullen* Banks, *Virtue Betrayed: or, Anna Bullen* (1682).
2 *Mr. Tate* Nahum Tate in *Injured Love: or, The Cruel Husband* (1707); *Gloriana* By Lee (1676).
3 *Cleom.* Dryden, *Cleomenes, The Spartan Hero* (1692).
4 *Victim* By Charles Johnson (1714).

KING. Thy modesty's a ^t candle to thy merit,
    It shines itself, and shows thy merit too.
10   But say, my boy, where did'st thou leave the giants?
TOM THUMB. My Liege, without° the castle gates they   *outside*
    stand,
    The castle gates too low for their admittance.
KING. What look they like?
TOM THUMB.   Like nothing but themselves.
15 QUEEN. (*Aside.*) ^u And sure thou art like nothing but thy self.
KING. Enough! the vast idea fills my soul.
    I see them, yes, I see them now before me:
    The monstrous, ugly, barb'rous sons of whores.
    But, ha! What form majestic strikes our eyes?
20   ^v So perfect that it seems to have been drawn
    By all the Gods in council: So fair she is,
    That surely at her birth the council paused,
    And then at length cried out, "This is a Woman!"
TOM THUMB. Then were the Gods mistaken. She is not
25   A woman, but a giantess—whom we
    ^w With much ado, have made a shift to haul
    Within the town ^x: for she is, by a foot,
    Shorter than all her subject giants were.
GLUMDALCA. We yesterday were both a queen and wife,
30   One hundred thousand giants owned our sway,[1]
    Twenty whereof were married to our self.
QUEEN. Oh! happy state of giantism—where husbands
    Like mushrooms grow, whilst hapless we are forced
    To be content, nay, happy thought with one.

---

1 *owned our sway* Our sovereign power possessed.

ᵗ We find a candlestick for this candle in two celebrated authors;
────────Each star withdraws
His golden head and burns within the socket.   *Nero.*[1]
A soul grown old and sunk into the socket.   *Sebastian.*

ᵘ This simile occurs very frequently among the dramatic writers of both kinds.

ᵛ Mr. Lee hath stolen this thought from our author;
────This perfect face, drawn by the gods in council,
Which they were long a making.   *Lu. Jun. Brut.*
────At his birth, the heavenly council paused,
And then at last cried out, this is a man!
Dryden hath improved this hint to the utmost perfection:
So perfect, that the very gods who formed you, wondered
At their own skill, and cried, a lucky hit
Has mended our design! Their envy hindered,
Or you had been immortal, and a pattern,
When heaven would work for ostentation sake,
To copy out again.   *All for Love.*
Banks prefers the works of Michelangelo to that of the gods;
A pattern for the gods to make a man by,
Or Michelangelo to form a statue.[2]

ʷ It is impossible, says Mr. W────,[3] sufficiently to admire this natural easy line.

ˣ This tragedy, which in most points resembles the ancients, differs from them in this: that it assigns the same honour to lowness of stature which they did to height. The gods and heroes in Homer and Virgil are continually described higher by the head than their followers, the contrary of which is observed by our author. In short, to exceed on either side is equally admirable, and a man of three foot is as wonderful a sight as a man of nine.

---

1 *Nero* By Lee (1675).
2 *Lu. Jun. Brut* Lee, *Lucius Junius Brutus; Father of his Country* (1680); *At his birth … this is a man!* from Lee and Dryden, *The Duke of Guise* (1683); *All for Love* By Dryden (1678); *A pattern … a statue* From Banks, *The Earl of Essex.*
3 *Mr. W──* The identity of Mr. W──remains uncertain, but the note might refer to poet and critic Leonard Welsted (1688–1747), who wrote effusively about poetical spirit and easy grace, and who was ridiculed by Pope in both *Peri Bathous* and *The Dunciad Variorum.*

35 GLUMDALCA. But then to lose them all in one black day,
      That the same sun, which rising, saw me wife
      To twenty giants, setting, should behold
      Me widowed of them all. ^y My worn out heart,
      That ship, leaks fast, and the great heavy lading,°   *cargo*
40   My soul, will quickly sink.
    QUEEN.   Madam, believe,
      I view your sorrows with a woman's eye;
      But learn to bear them with what strength you may,
      Tomorrow we will have our grenadiers[1]
45   Drawn out before you, and you then shall choose
      What husbands you think fit.
    GLUMDALCA.   ^z Madam, I am
      Your most obedient, and most humble servant.
    KING. Think, mighty princess, think this court your own,
50   Nor think the landlord me, this house my inn;
      Call for whate'er you will, you'll nothing pay.
      ^{aa} I feel a sudden pain within my breast,
      Nor know I whether it arise from love,
      Or only the wind-colic.[2] Time must show.
55   Oh, Thumb! What do we to thy valour owe?
      Ask some reward, great as we can bestow.
    TOM THUMB. ^{bb} I ask not kingdoms, I can conquer those,
      I ask not money, money I've enough;
      For what I've done, and what I mean to do,
60   For giants slain, and giants yet unborn,
      Which I will slay—if this be called a debt,
      Take my receipt in full—I ask but this,
      ^{cc} To sun myself in Huncamunca's eyes.
    KING. (*Aside.*) Prodigious bold request.
65 QUEEN. (*Aside.*)   ^{dd} Be still my soul.
    TOM THUMB. ^{ee} My heart is at the threshold of your mouth,
      And waits its answer there—Oh! do not frown,
      I've tried, to reason's tune, to tune my soul,
      But love did over-wind and crack the string.

---

1 *grenadiers* Tallest and best soldiers in a regiment.
2 *wind-colic* Colic (stomach pains) caused by gas.

^y My blood leaks fast, and the great heavy lading
My soul will quickly sink.   *Mithrid.*
My soul is like a ship.   *Injured Love.*

^z This well-bred line seems to be copied in *The Persian Princess*;
To be your humblest, and most faithful slave.

^{aa} This doubt of the King puts me in mind of a passage in *The Captives*,
where the noise of feet is mistaken for the rustling of leaves,
————Methinks I hear
The sound of feet. [...]
No, 'twas the wind that shook yon cypress boughs.

^{bb} Mr. Dryden seems to have had this passage in his eye in the first page of
Love Triumphant.[1]

^{cc} Don Carlos in *The Revenge* suns himself in the charms of his mistress,
While in the lustre of her charms I lay.

^{dd} A tragical phrase much in use.

^{ee} This speech hath been taken to pieces by several tragical authors who seem
to have rifled it and shared its beauties among them.
My soul waits at the portal of thy breast,
To ravish from thy lips the welcome news.   *Anna Bullen.*
My soul stands listening at my ears.   *Cyrus the Great.*
Love to his tune my jarring heart would bring,
But reason overwinds and cracks the string.   *D. of Guise.*
————I should have loved,
Though Jove in muttering thunder had   New *Sophonisba.*
forbid it.
And when it (my Heart) wild resolves to love no more,
Then is the triumph of excessive love.   *Ibidem.*[2]

---

1   *Love Triumphant* Dryden, *Love Triumphant: or, Nature Will Prevail* (1694). Fielding
seems to have cited the wrong play; he probably means to refer to *The Indian Queen*
(1665), a heroic play by Dryden and Robert Howard in which the ruler of the Incas offers
a reward to his general, who asks to marry the princess.
2   *Ibidem.* Latin: "in the same place."

70   Though Jove[1] in thunder had cried out, YOU SHAN'T,
    I should have loved her still—for oh, strange fate,
    Then when I loved her least, I loved her most.
    KING. It is resolved—the Princess is your own.
    TOM THUMB. ^{ff} Oh! happy, happy, happy, happy, Thumb!
75   QUEEN. Consider, sir, reward your soldier's merit,
    But give not Huncamunca to Tom Thumb.
    KING. Tom Thumb! Odzooks,[2] my wide extended realm
    Knows not a name so glorious as Tom Thumb.
    Let Macedonia, Alexander boast,
80   Let Rome her Caesars and her Scipios show,
    Her Messieurs France, let Holland boast Mynheers,
    Ireland her Os, her Macs let Scotland boast,
    Let England boast no other than Tom Thumb.[3]
    QUEEN. Though greater yet his boasted merit was,
85   He shall not have my daughter, that is pos'.°   *positive*
    KING. Ha! sayest thou Dollalolla?
    QUEEN.   .   I say he shan't.
    KING. ^{gg} Then by our royal self we swear you lie.
    QUEEN. ^{hh} Who but a dog, who but a dog,
90   Would use me as thou dost? Me, who have lain
    ⁱⁱ These twenty years so loving by thy side.
    But I will be revenged. I'll hang myself,
    Then tremble all who did this match persuade,
    ^{jj} For riding on a cat,[4] from high I'll fall,
95   And squirt down royal vengeance on you all.
    FOODLE. ^{kk} Her Majesty the Queen is in a passion.
    KING. ^{ll} Be she, or be she not—I'll to the girl
    And pave thy way, oh Thumb—Now, by our self,

---

1   *Jove* In Roman mythology, father of the gods.
2   *Odzooks* Expression of surprise euphemistically substituting "od" for "god."
3   *Alexander* Alexander the Great, Greek king of Macedon in the fourth century BCE; *Caesars* Refers to Julius Caesar, legendary Roman general of the first century BCE; *Scipios* Refers to Scipio Africanus, a Roman general who defeated Hannibal in the Second Punic War (in 202 BCE); *Messieurs* French form of polite address, equivalent to "Misters"; *Mynheers* The Dutch equivalent of "Messieurs"; *Os* I.e., surnames starting with "O," common in Ireland and meaning "son of"; *Macs* Surnames starting with "Mac," common in Scotland and meaning "son of."
4   *cat* Moveable structure used in sieges.

ff Massinissa is one fourth less happy than Tom Thumb.
Oh! happy, happy, happy. New *Sophonisba.*

gg No by my self.¹ *Anna Bullen.*

hh —————Who caused
This dreadful revolution in my fate?
ULAMAR. Who but a dog, who but a dog. *Liberty Asserted.*

ii —————A bride,
Who twenty years lay loving by your side. Banks.²

jj For borne upon a cloud, from high I'll fall,
And rain down royal vengeance on you all. *Albion Queen.*

kk An information very like this we have in *The Tragedy of Love*, where Cyrus
having stormed in the most violent manner, Cyaxares observes very calmly,
Why, nephew Cyrus—you are moved.

ll 'Tis in your choice,
Love me, or love me not! *Conquest of Granada.*³

---

1 *No by my self* In the quoted line, the speaker swears on his own person.
2 *Banks* In *Virtue Betrayed: or, Anna Bullen.*
3 *Conquest of Granada* In two parts, by Dryden (1672). These lines are actually from Dryden's *The Indian Emperor* (1667).

We were indeed a pretty king of clouts,
100   To truckle° to her will—For when by force   *submit*
Or art the wife her husband over-reaches,
Give him the petticoat, and her the breeches.
TOM THUMB. ᵐᵐ Whisper, ye winds, that Huncamunca's mine;
Echoes repeat that Huncamunca's mine!
105   The dreadful business of the war is o'er,
And beauty, heavenly beauty! crowns my toils,
I've thrown the bloody garment now aside,
And hymeneal° sweets invite my bride.   *marital*
So when some chimney-sweeper, all the day,
110   Hath through dark paths pursued the sooty way,
At night, to wash his hands and face he flies,
And in his t'other shirt with his Brickdusta lies.

ACT I, SCENE 4

(*Grizzle solus.*)[1]

GRIZZLE. ⁿⁿ Where art thou Grizzle? where are now thy glories?
Where are the drums that wakened thee to honour?
Greatness is a laced coat from Monmouth Street,
Which Fortune lends us for a day to wear,
5   Tomorrow puts it on another's back.
The spiteful sun but yesterday surveyed
His rival, high as Saint Paul's cupola;
Now may he see me as Fleet-Ditch laid low.[2]

---

1   *solus* Latin: alone.
2   *Monmouth Street* Location of many used-clothing stores in eighteenth-century London; *Saint Paul's cupola* The dome of St. Paul's Cathedral, one of the most admired
works of architecture of the time; *Fleet-Ditch* Colloquial name for the Fleet River,
which ran down into the Thames at Blackfriars Bridge and which was transformed
by pollution into an open sewer—a low point, topographically and culturally.

mm There is not one beauty in this charming speech but hath been borrowed by almost every tragic writer.

nn Mr. Banks has (I wish I could not say too servilely) imitated this of Grizzle in his *Earl of Essex.*

  Where art thou Essex, &c.[1]

---

1 *Where art thou Essex, &c.* The original lines from *The Earl of Essex* are parodied at length
 in Grizzle's soliloquy:
  Where art thou Essex! Where are now thy Glories! ...
  The early songs that every morning waked thee; ...
  Yesterday's sun saw his great rival thus,
  The spiteful planet saw me thus adored,
  And some tall-built pyramid, whose height
  And golden top confronts him in his sky
  He tumbles down with lightning in his rage
  So on a sudden he has snatched my garlands.

ACT 1, Scene 5

(*Queen, Grizzle.*)

QUEEN. °° Teach me to scold, prodigious-minded Grizzle.
Mountain of treason, ugly as the devil,
Teach this confounded hateful mouth of mine
To spout forth words malicious as thyself,
5   Words which might shame all Billingsgate[1] to speak.
GRIZZLE. Far be it from my pride to think my tongue
Your royal lips can in that art instruct,
Wherein you so excel. But may I ask,
Without offence, wherefore my Queen would scold?
10   QUEEN. Wherefore, oh! Blood and thunder! han't you heard
(What every corner of the court resounds)
That little Thumb will be a great man[2] made.
GRIZZLE. I heard it, I confess—for who, alas!
PP Can always stop his ears—but would my teeth,
15   By grinding knives, had first been set on edge.
QUEEN. Would I had heard at the still noon of night,[3]
The hallaloo[4] of fire in every street!
Odsbobs! I have a mind to hang myself,
To think I should a grandmother be made,
20   By such a rascal. Sure the King forgets,
When in a pudding, by his mother put,
The bastard, by a tinker, on a stile°   *window frame*
Was dropped.—O, good Lord Grizzle! can I bear
To see him, from a pudding, mount the throne?
25   Or can, oh can! my Huncamunca bear,
To take a pudding's offspring to her arms?

---

1   *Billingsgate* Area of London by the Thames where the fishmongers lived; the reference is to the proverbially sharp tongues of fishwives.
2   *great man* Possibly a satiric swipe at Robert Walpole, England's chief minister
through the 1730s, who was sarcastically referred to as a "Great Man," and who was
responsible for the Stage Licensing Act of 1737, which effectively ended Fielding's
dramatic career.
3   *noon of night* Midnight.
4   *hallaloo* Cry to come help.

ᵒᵒ The Countess of Nottingham in *The Earl of Essex* is apparently acquainted with Dollalolla.[1]

ᵖᵖ Grizzle was not probably possessed of that glue, of which Mr. Banks speaks in his *Cyrus*.

I'll glue my ears to ev'ry word.

---

1   *The Countess of Nottingham* The implication is that Banks's character borrows her well-known complaint from Dollalolla:

> Help me to rail, prodigious minded Burleigh,
> Prince of bold English councils, teach me how
> This hateful breast of mine may dart forth words
> Keen as thy wit, malicious as thy person.

GRIZZLE. Oh horror! horror! horror! cease my Queen,
   qq Thy voice, like twenty screech-owls, wracks my brain.
QUEEN. Then rouse thy spirit—we may yet prevent
30   This hated match—
GRIZZLE.   We will rr; not fate itself,
   Should it conspire with Thomas Thumb, should cause it.
   I'll swim through seas; I'll ride upon the clouds;
   I'll dig the earth; I'll blow out ev'ry fire;
35   I'll rave; I'll rant; I'll rise; I'll rush; I'll roar;
   Fierce as the man whom ss smiling dolphins bore,
   From the prosaic to poetic shore.
   I'll tear the scoundrel into twenty pieces.
QUEEN. Oh, no! prevent the match, but hurt him not;
40   For though I would not have him have my daughter,
   Yet can we kill the man that killed the giants?
GRIZZLE. I tell you, madam, it was all a trick.
   He made the giants first, and then he killed them;
   As fox hunters bring foxes to the wood,
45   And then with hounds they drive them out again.
QUEEN. How! have you seen no giants? Are there not
   Now, in the yard, ten thousand proper giants?
GRIZZLE. tt Indeed, I cannot positively tell,
   But firmly do believe there is not one.
50   QUEEN. Hence! from my sight! thou traitor, hie° away;   *go*
   By all my stars! Thou enviest Tom Thumb.
   Go, sirrah! go, uu hie away! hie!—thou art
   A setting dog, be gone.
GRIZZLE.   Madam, I go.
55   Tom Thumb shall feel the vengeance you have raised:
   So, when two dogs are fighting in the streets,
   With a third dog one of the two dogs meets,
   With angry teeth he bites him to the bone,
   And this dog smarts for what that dog had done.

qq Screech-owls, dark ravens and amphibious monsters,
Are screaming in that voice. *Mary Q. of Scots.*

rr The reader may see all the beauties of this speech in a late ode called the *Naval Lyric.*[1]

ss This epithet to a dolphin doth not give one so clear an idea as were to be wished, a smiling fish seeming a little more difficult to be imagined than a flying fish. Mr. Dryden is of opinion, that smiling is the property of reason, and that no irrational creature can smile.

Smiles not allowed to beasts from reason *State of Innocence.*
move.

tt These lines are written in the same key with those in *The Earl of Essex*;
Why say'st thou so, I love thee well, indeed
I do, and thou shalt find by this, 'tis true.
Or with this in *Cyrus*;
The most heroic mind that ever was.
And with above half of the modern tragedies.

uu Aristotle in that excellent work of his which is very justly styled his masterpiece, earnestly recommends using the terms of art, however coarse or even indecent they may be.[2] Mr. Tate is of the same opinion.
BRACHIANO. Do not, like young hawks, fetch a course about,
Your game flies fair.
FRANCISCO. Do not fear it.
He answers you in your own hawking phrase. *Injured Love.*
I think these two great authorities are sufficient to justify Dollalolla in the use of the phrase "hie away hie" when in the same line she says she is speaking to a setting dog.

---

1 *Naval Lyric* Young's *Imperium Pelagi* (*Empire of the Sea*): *A Naval Lyric* (1730) makes extensive use of alliteration and repetition. It also mentions a smiling dolphin.
2 *masterpiece* An imaginary citation from Aristotle's *Poetics*, which contains no such recommendation. Given the privileging of the "indecent," there may also be a pun on "*Aristotle's Masterpiece*," a notorious manual of sex that circulated in the late seventeenth and eighteenth century. Its authorship is unclear.

ACT 1, Scene 6

(*Queen sola.*)

QUEEN. And whither shall I go? Alack-a-day!
I love Tom Thumb—but must not tell him so;
For what's a woman, when her virtue's gone?
A coat without its lace; wig out of buckle;
5   A stocking with a hole in't—I can't live
Without my virtue, or without Tom Thumb.
ᵥᵥ Then let me weigh them in two equal scales,
In this scale put my virtue, that, Tom Thumb.
Alas! Tom Thumb is heavier than my virtue.
10   But hold!—perhaps I may be left a widow:
This match prevented, then Tom Thumb is mine:
In that dear hope, I will forget my pain.
So, when some wench to Tothill-Bridewell's sent,
With beating hemp, and flogging[1] she's content:
15   She hopes in time to ease her present pain,
At length is free, and walks the streets again.

ACT 2, Scene 1. The street.

(*Bailiff, Follower.*)

BAILIFF. Come on, my trusty follower, come on,
This day discharge thy duty, and at night
A double mug of beer, and beer shall glad thee.
Stand here by me, this way must Noodle pass.
5   FOLLOWER. No more, no more, oh bailiff! every word
Inspires my soul with virtue.—Oh! I long
To meet the enemy in the street—and nab him;
To lay arresting hands upon his back,
And drag him trembling to the sponging-house.[2]

---

1   *Tothill-Bridewell* Prison in London; *beating hemp* Work for women prisoners sentenced to hard labor; *flogging* Typical punishment for prisoners who did not work hard enough.
2   *sponging-house* Bailiff's house, where suspected criminals would be held until their trial.

ᵛᵛ We meet with such another pair of scales in Dryden's *King Arthur*.

Arthur and Oswald, and their different fates,
Are weighing now within the scales of heav'n.

Also in *Sebastian*.

This hour my lot is weighing in the scales.

10 BAILIFF. There, when I have him, I will sponge upon him.[1]
ww Oh! glorious thought! By the sun, moon, and stars,
I will enjoy it, though it be in thought!
Yes, yes, my follower, I will enjoy it.
FOLLOWER. Enjoy it then some other time, for now
15 Our prey approaches.
BAILIFF. Let us retire.

ACT 2, SCENE 2

(*Tom Thumb, Noodle, Bailiff, Follower.*)

TOM THUMB. Trust me my Noodle, I am wondrous sick;
For though I love the gentle Huncamunca,
Yet at the thought of marriage, I grow pale;
For oh!— xx but swear thoul't keep it ever secret,
5 I will unfold a tale will make thee stare.
NOODLE. I swear by lovely Huncamunca's charms.
TOM THUMB. Then know — yy my grand-mamma hath often said,
Tom Thumb, beware of marriage.
NOODLE.   Sir, I blush
10 To think a warrior great in arms as you
Should be affrighted by his grand-mamma;
Can an old woman's empty dreams deter
The blooming hero from the virgin's arms?
Think of the joy that will your soul alarm,°   *rouse, excite*
15 When in her fond embraces clasped you lie,
While on her panting breast dissolved in bliss,
You pour out all Tom Thumb in every kiss.
TOM THUMB. Oh! Noodle, thou hast fired my eager soul;
Spite° of my grandmother, she shall be mine;   *in spite*
20 I'll hug, caress, I'll eat her up with love.
Whole days, and nights, and years shall be too short
For our enjoyment, every sun shall rise
zz Blushing, to see us in our bed together.
NOODLE. Oh, sir! this purpose of your soul pursue.

---

1   *sponge upon him* Press him for money; force him to pay for his keep.

ᵂᵂ Mr. Rowe is generally imagined to have taken some hints from this scene in his character of Bajazet;[1] but as he, of all the tragic writers, bears the least resemblance to our author in his diction, I am unwilling to imagine he would condescend to copy him in this particular.

ˣˣ This method of surprising an audience by raising their expectation to the highest pitch, and then baulking it, hath been practised with great success by most of our tragical authors.

ʸʸ Almeyda in *Sebastian* is in the same distress;
Sometimes methinks I hear the groan of ghosts,
Thin hollow sounds and lamentable screams;
Then, like a dying echo from afar,
My mother's voice that cries, wed not Almeyda!
Forewarned, Almeyda, marriage is thy crime.

ᶻᶻ As very well he may if he hath any modesty in him, says Mr. D——s. The Author of *Busiris* is extremely zealous to prevent the sun's blushing at any indecent object; and therefore on all such occasions he addresses himself to the sun, and desires him to keep out of the way.
Rise never more, O sun! let night prevail,
Eternal darkness close the world's wide scene.   *Busiris.*
Sun hide thy face and put the world in mourning.   *Ibid.*
Mr. Banks makes the sun perform the office of Hymen; and therefore not likely to be disgusted at such a sight:
The sun sets forth like a gay brideman[2] with   *Mary Q. of Scots.*
you.

---

1   *Bajazet* In Act II of *Tamerlane*, the villain Bajazet exclaims: "Oh, glorious thought! by heav'n I will enjoy it, / Though but in fancy."
2   *brideman* Bridegroom's attendant.

25 BAILIFF. Oh, sir! I have an action against you.
NOODLE. At whose suit is it?
BAILIFF.   At your tailor's, sir.
  Your tailor put this warrant in my hands,
  And I arrest you, sir, at his commands.
30 TOM THUMB. Ha! Dogs! Arrest my friend before my face!
  Think you Tom Thumb will suffer this disgrace!
  But let vain cowards threaten by their word,
  Tom Thumb shall show his anger by his sword.

(*Kills the Bailiff and his Follower.*)

BAILIFF. Oh, I am slain!
35 FOLLOWER.   I am murdered also,
  And to the shades, the dismal shades below,
  My bailiff's faithful follower, I go.
NOODLE. [aaa] Go then to Hell, like rascals as you are,
  And give our service to the bailiffs there.
40 TOM THUMB. Thus perish all the bailiffs in the land,
  Till debtors at noon-day shall walk the streets,
  And no one fear a bailiff or his writ.

ACT 2, SCENE 3. THE PRINCESS HUNCAMUNCA'S APARTMENT.

(*Huncamunca, Cleora, Mustacha.*)

HUNCAMUNCA. [bbb] Give me some music—see that it be sad.
CLEORA. (*Sings.*) Cupid, ease a love-sick maid,
  Bring thy quiver to her aid;
  With equal ardour wound the swain:°   *sweetheart*
5 Beauty should never sigh in vain.
  Let him feel the pleasing smart,
  Drive thy arrow through his heart;
  When one you wound, you then destroy;
  When both you kill, you kill with joy.
10 HUNCAMUNCA. [ccc] O, Tom Thumb! Tom Thumb! wherefore art
      thou Tom Thumb?
  Why had'st thou not been born of royal race?

^{aaa} Nourmahal sends the same message to Heaven;
    For I would have you, when you upwards move,
    Speak kindly of us to our friends above.   *Aureng-Zebe.*
We find another to Hell, in *The Persian Princess*;
    Villain, get thee down
    To Hell, and tell them that the fray's begun.

^{bbb} Anthony gives the same command in the same words.[1]

^{ccc} Oh! Marius, Marius; wherefore art thou Marius?   Otway's *Marius.*[2]

---

1 *Anthony* In Dryden's *All for Love.*
2 *Otway's Marius The History and Fall of Caius Marius* borrows heavily from *Romeo and Juliet,* although Shakespeare's play had not been mounted on the London stage since the early 1660s. Part of the joke is that, for all his pedantry, Scriblerus Secundus is blind to obvious Shakespearean allusion.

Why had not mighty Bantam[1] been thy father?
Or else the King of Brentford, old or new?[2]

MUSTACHA. I am surprised that your Highness can give yourself
a moment's uneasiness about that little insignificant fellow, ᵈᵈᵈ
Tom Thumb the Great—One properer for a play-thing, than a
husband. Were he my husband, his horns should be as long as
his body. If you had fallen in love with a grenadier, I should not
have wondered at it—If you had fallen in love with something;
but to fall in love with nothing!

HUNCAMUNCA. Cease, my Mustacha, on thy duty cease.
The zephyr,° when in flow'ry vales it plays,   *west wind*
Is not so soft, so sweet as Thummy's breath.
The dove is not so gentle to its mate.

MUSTACHA. The dove is every bit as proper for a husband—Alas!
Madam, there's not a beau about the court looks so little like a
man—He is a perfect butterfly, a thing without substance, and
almost without shadow too.

HUNCAMUNCA. This rudeness is unseasonable, desist;
Or, I shall think this railing° comes from love.   *complaining*
Tom Thumb's a creature of that charming form,
That no one can abuse, unless they love him.

MUSTACHA. Madam, the King.

ACT 2, SCENE 4

KING. Let all but Huncamunca leave the room.

(*Exit Cleora and Mustacha.*)

---

1   *Bantam* In Fielding's earlier play, *The Author's Farce* (1730), the impecunious poet
    and playwright Luckless is relieved of his woes when he is implausibly discovered to
    be the lost heir to the throne of Bantam, a center of trade in the northwest of Java
    that had long signified exotic opulence.
2   *King of ... new* Brentford was a proverbially squalid village west of London, in which
    it was said two rival kings (the "old" and "new") quarreled over succession. Fielding
    alludes to the play-within-a-play in his burlesque predecessor, Buckingham's *The Re-
    hearsal* (1671), which takes the attempted usurpation of the Kingdom of Brentford
    as its subject.

ddd Nothing is more common than these seeming contradictions; such as,
Haughty weakness. *Victim.*
Great small world. *Noah's Flood.*[1]

---

1   *Noah's Flood* By Edward Ecclestone (1679).

Daughter, I have observed of late some grief,
Unusual in your countenance—your eyes,
eee That, like two open windows, used to show
5   The lovely beauty of the rooms within,
Have now two blinds before them—What is the cause?
Say, have you not enough of meat and drink?
We've given strict orders not to have you stinted.
HUNCAMUNCA. Alas! my Lord, I value not myself,
10   That once I eat two fowls and half a pig;
fff Small is that praise; but oh! a maid may want,
What she can neither eat nor drink.
KING.   What's that?
HUNCAMUNCA. ggg O spare my blushes; but I mean a husband.
15 KING. If that be all, I have provided one,
A husband great in arms, whose warlike sword
Streams with the yellow blood of slaughtered giants.
Whose name in *terra incognita*[1] is known,
Whose valour, wisdom, virtue make a noise,
20   Great as the kettle-drums of twenty armies.
HUNCAMUNCA. Whom does my royal father mean?
KING. Tom Thumb.
HUNCAMUNCA. Is it possible?
KING. Ha! the window-blinds are gone,
25   hhh A country dance of joy is in your face,
Your eyes spit fire, your cheeks grow red as beef.
HUNCAMUNCA. O, there's a magic music in that sound,
Enough to turn me into beef indeed.
Yes, I will own, since licensed by your word,
30   I'll own Tom Thumb the cause of all my grief.
For him I've sighed, I've wept, I've gnawed my sheets.
KING. Oh! thou shalt gnaw thy tender sheets no more,
A husband thou shalt have to mumble now.
HUNCAMUNCA. Oh! happy sound! henceforth, let no one tell,
35   That Huncamunca shall lead apes in Hell.[2]
Oh! I am overjoyed!

---

1   *terra incognita* Latin: unknown territory.
2   *lead apes in Hell* The proverbial fate of unmarried women.

^{eee} Lee hath improved this metaphor.
> Dost thou not view joy peeping from my eyes,
> The casements opened wide to gaze on thee;
> So Rome's glad citizens to windows rise,
> When they some young triumpher fain would see. *Gloriana.*

^{fff} Almahide hath the same contempt for these appetites;
> To eat and drink can no perfection be. *Conquest of Granada.*

The Earl of Essex is of a different opinion, and seems to place the chief happiness of a General therein.
> Were but commanders half so well rewarded,
> Then they might eat. Banks's *Earl of Essex.*

But if we may believe one who knows more than either—the Devil himself—we shall find eating to be an affair of more moment than is generally imagined.
> Gods are immortal only by
> their food. Lucifer in *The State of Innocence.*

^{ggg} This expression is enough of itself (says Mr. D——s) utterly to destroy the character of Huncamunca; yet we find a woman of no abandoned character in Dryden, adventuring farther and thus excusing herself;
> To speak our wishes first, forbid it pride,
> Forbid it modesty: true, they forbid it,
> But nature does not, when we are athirst
> Or hungry, will imperious nature stay,
> Nor eat, nor drink, before 'tis bid fall on. *Cleomenes.*

Cassandra speaks before she is asked. Huncamunca afterwards. Cassandra speaks her wishes to her lover, Huncamunca only to her father.

^{hhh} Her eyes resistless magic bear,
> Angels I see, and gods are dancing there. Lee's *Sophonisba.*

KING.   I see thou art.
[iii] Joy lightens in thy eyes, and thunders from thy brows;
Transports,° like lightning, dart along thy soul,   *fits of ecstasy*
40   As small-shot° through a hedge.   *musket bullets*
HUNCAMUNCA.   Oh! say not small.
KING.   This happy news shall on our tongue ride post,[1]
Our self will bear the happy news to Thumb.
Yet think not, daughter, that your powerful charms
45   Must still detain the hero from his arms;
Various his duty, various his delight;
Now is his turn to kiss, and now to fight;
And now to kiss again. So mighty [jjj] Jove,
When with excessive thundering tired above,
50   Comes down to earth, and takes a bit[2]—and then,
Flies to his trade of thundering, back again.

ACT 2, SCENE 5

(*Grizzle, Huncamunca.*)

[kkk] GRIZZLE.   Oh, Huncamunca, Huncamunca, oh,
Thy pouting breasts, like kettle-drums of brass,
Beat everlasting loud alarms of joy;
As bright as brass they are, and oh, as hard;
5   Oh Huncamunca, Huncamunca! oh!
HUNCAMUNCA.   Ha! do'st thou know me, princess as I am,
[lll] That thus of me you dare to make your game.
GRIZZLE.   Oh Huncamunca, well I know that you
A princess are, and a king's daughter too.
10   But love no meanness scorns, no grandeur fears,
Love often lords into the cellar bears,
And bids the sturdy porter come upstairs.
For what's too high for love, or what's too low?
Oh Huncamunca, Huncamunca, oh!

---

1   *ride post* Practice of carrying mail with the greatest possible speed, stopping at each
    interval, or post, along the road only to change to a fresh horse.
2   *So mighty Jove ... a bit* In Roman mythology, Jove would often assume the form of
    some animal and, in that form, rape a mortal woman.

iii Mr. Dennis in that excellent tragedy called *Liberty Asserted*, which is thought to have given so great a stroke to the late French King,[1] hath frequent imitations of this beautiful speech of King Arthur;
> Conquest lightning in his eyes, and thund'ring in his arm.
> Joy lightened in her eyes.
> Joys like lightning dart along my soul.

jjj Jove with excessive thund'ring tired above,
> Comes down for ease, enjoys a nymph, and then
> Mounts dreadful, and to thund'ring goes again.   *Gloriana.*

kkk This beautiful Line, which ought, says Mr. W——, to be written in gold, is imitated in the new *Sophonisba*;
> Oh! Sophonisba, Sophonisba, oh!
> Oh! Narva, Narva, oh!

The author of a song called *Duke upon Duke*,[2] hath improved it:
> Alas! O Nick, O Nick, alas!

Where, by the help of a little false spelling, you have two meanings in the repeated words.

lll Edith, in *The Bloody Brother*,[3] speaks to her lover in the same familiar language.
> Your grace is full of game.

---

1   *Liberty Asserted ... French King* It was said that Dennis so greatly overestimated the political impact of his anti-French play that he feared abduction by the French government.
2   *Duke upon Duke* A 1720 broadside ballad, partly written by Pope, commemorating a quarrel between Sir John Guise (1677–1732) and Nicholas Lechmere (1675–1727).
3   *The Bloody Brother* By John Fletcher, Phillip Massinger, and others (1639).

15   HUNCAMUNCA. But granting all you say of love were true,
     My love, alas! is to another due!
     In vain, to me a-suitoring you come;
     For I'm already promised to Tom Thumb.
     GRIZZLE. And can my princess such a durgen° wed,   *dwarf*
20   One fitter for your pocket than your bed!
     Advised by me, the worthless baby shun,
     Or you will ne'er be brought to bed of one.
     Oh take me to thy arms and never flinch,
     Who am a man by Jupiter ev'ry inch.
25   [mmm] Then while in joys together lost we lie
     I'll press thy soul while gods stand wishing by.
     HUNCAMUNCA. If, sir, what you insinuate you prove,
     All obstacles of promise you remove;
     For all engagements to a man must fall,
30   Whene'er that man is proved no man at all.
     GRIZZLE. Oh let him seek some dwarf, some fairy miss,
     Where no joint-stool[1] must lift him to the kiss.
     But by the stars and glory, you appear
     Much fitter for a Prussian grenadier;
35   One globe alone on Atlas'[2] shoulders rests,
     Two globes are less than Huncamunca's breasts:
     The milky way is not so white, that's flat,
     And sure thy breasts are full as large as that.
     HUNCAMUNCA. Oh, sir, so strong your eloquence I find,
40   It is impossible to be unkind.
     GRIZZLE. Ah! speak that o'er again, and let the [nnn] sound
     From one pole to another pole rebound;
     The earth and sky each be a battledore[3]
     And keep the sound, that shuttlecock, up an hour;
45   To Doctors Commons[4] for a license I,
     Swift as an arrow from a bow, will fly.

---

1 *joint-stool* High rectangular seat common around eighteenth-century dinner tables.
2 *Atlas* Ancient god who supposedly held up the pillars of the universe.
3 *battledore* Racket used in playing "battledore and shuttlecock," an early version of bad-
   minton in which two players hit a shuttlecock, a cork with feathers attached to it, back and
   forth without letting it drop.
4 *Doctors Commons* College for lawyers where one could get a marriage license quickly.

[mmm] Traverse the glitt'ring chambers of the sky,
Borne on a cloud in view of fate I'll lie,
And press her soul while gods stand wishing by.   *Hannibal.* [1]

[nnn] Let the four winds from distant corners meet,
And on their wings first bear it into France;
Then back again to Edina's proud walls,
Till victim to the sound th'aspiring city falls.   *Albion Queens.*

---

1   *Hannibal* Alternate title of Lee's *Sophonisba.*

HUNCAMUNCA. Oh no! lest some disaster we should meet,
'Twere better to be married at the Fleet.[1]
GRIZZLE. Forbid it, all ye powers, a princess should
50   By that vile place contaminate her blood;
My quick return shall to my charmer prove,
I travel on the ᵒᵒᵒ post-horses[2] of love.
HUNCAMUNCA. Those post-horses to me will seem too slow,
Though they should fly swift as the gods, when they
55   Ride on behind that post-boy, opportunity.

ACT 2, Scene 6

(*Tom Thumb, Huncamunca.*)

TOM THUMB. Where is my Princess, where's my Huncamunca?
Where are those eyes, those cardmatches[3] of love,
That ᴾᴾᴾ light up all with love my waxen soul?
Where is that face which artful nature made
5   ۹۹۹ In the same moulds where Venus' self was cast?

---

1 *married at the Fleet* I.e., married in secret, without a license, by a disreputable clergy-
man (such as one imprisoned in the Fleet Street prison).
2 *post-horses* Horses kept for riding post.
3 *cardmatches* Pieces of card dipped in melted sulphur.

ooo I do not remember any metaphors so frequent in the tragic poets as those borrowed from riding post;

The gods and opportunity ride post. *Hannibal.*
———Let's rush together,
For death rides post. *Duke of Guise.*[1]
Destruction gallops to thy murder post. *Gloriana.*

ppp This image too very often occurs;

———Bright as when thy eye
First lighted up our loves. *Aureng-Zebe.*
This not a crown alone lights up my name. *Busiris.*

qqq There is great dissension among the poets concerning the method of making man. One tells his mistress that the mould she was made in being lost, Heaven cannot form such another. Lucifer in Dryden gives a merry description of his own formation;

Whom Heaven neglecting, made and scarce designed,
But threw me in for number to the rest. *State of Innocence.*

In one place, the same poet supposes man to be made of metal;

I was formed
Of that coarse metal, which when she was made,
The gods threw by for rubbish. *All for Love.*

In another, of dough;

When the gods moulded up the paste of man,
Some of their clay was left upon their hands,
And so they made Egyptians. *Cleomenes.*

In another of clay;

———Rubbish of remaining clay. *Sebastian.*

One makes the soul of wax;

Her waxen soul begins to melt apace. *Anna Bullen.*

Another of flint;

Sure our two souls have somewhere been acquainted
In former beings, or struck out together,
One spark to Afric flew, and one to Portugal. *Sebastian.*

To omit the great quantities of iron, brazen and leaden souls which are so plenty in modern authors—I cannot omit the dress of a soul as we find it in Dryden;

Souls shirted but with air. *King Arthur.*

(continued)

---

1 *Duke of Guise* These lines actually appear in Lee's *Caesar Borgia.*

HUNCAMUNCA. [rrr] Oh! What is music to the ear that's deaf,
Or a goose-pie to him that has no taste?
What are these praises now to me, since I
Am promised to another?
10 TOM THUMB.   Ha! promised.
HUNCAMUNCA. Too sure; it's written in the book of fate.
TOM THUMB. [sss] Then I will tear away the leaf
Wherein it's writ, or if fate won't allow
So large a gap within its journal-book,
15 I'll blot it out at least.

ACT 2, Scene 7

(*Glumdalca, Tom Thumb, Huncamunca.*)

GLUMDALCA. [ttt] I need not ask if you are Huncamunca,
Your brandy nose[1] proclaims—
HUNCAMUNCA.   I am a princess;
Nor need I ask who you are.
5 GLUMDALCA.   A giantess;
The queen of those who made and unmade queens.
HUNCAMUNCA. The man whose chief ambition is to be
My sweetheart hath destroyed these mighty giants.
GLUMDALCA. Your sweetheart? dost thou think the man who
once
10 Hath worn my easy chains, will e'er wear thine?
HUNCAMUNCA. Well may your chains be easy, since if fame
Says true, they have been tried on twenty husbands.
[uuu] The glove or boot, so many times pulled on,
May well sit easy on the hand or foot.
15 GLUMDALCA. I glory in the number, and when I
Sit poorly down, like thee, content with one,
Heaven change this face for one as bad as thine.
HUNCAMUNCA. Let me see nearer what this beauty is
That captivates the heart of men by scores.°   *twenties*

---

1   *brandy nose* Enlarged and reddened nose with a deformed appearance, associated
with alcoholism.

Nor can I pass by a particular sort of soul in a particular sort of description, in the new *Sophonisba*.

> Ye mysterious powers,
> ——Whether through your gloomy depths I wander,
> Or on the mountains walk; give me the calm,
> The steady smiling soul, where wisdom sheds
> Eternal sunshine, and eternal joy.

ʳʳʳ This line Mr. Banks has plundered entire in his *Anna Bullen*.

ˢˢˢ Good Heaven, the Book of Fate before me lay,
But to tear out the journal of that day.
Or if the order of the world below,
Will not the gap of one whole day allow,
Give me that minute when she made   *Conquest of Granada.*
her vow.

ᵗᵗᵗ I know some of the commentators have imagined, that Mr. Dryden, in the altercative scene between Cleopatra and Octavia, a scene which Mr. Addison inveighs against with great bitterness,[1] is much beholden to our author. How just this their observation is, I will not presume to determine.

ᵘᵘᵘ A cobbling poet indeed, says Mr. D. and yet I believe we may find as monstrous images in the tragic authors: I'll put down one;
> Untie your folded thoughts, and let them dangle loose as a
> Bride's hair.   *Injured Love.*

Which lines seem to have as much title to a milliner's shop, as our author's to a shoemaker's.

---

1   *the altercative scene* The exchange between Cleopatra and Octavia, the romantic rivals for Anthony, appears in Act I Scene I of *All for Love*; *Mr. Addison* Addison had claimed in *The Guardian* No. 110 (17 July 1713) that anyone reading the scene would "be amazed to hear a Roman lady's mouth filled with such obscene raillery."

(Holds a candle to her face.)

20 Oh! Heaven, thou art as ugly as the devil.
GLUMDALCA. You'd give the best of shoes within your shop,
To be but half so handsome.
HUNCAMUNCA.   Since you come
ᵛᵛᵛ To that, I'll put my beauty to the test;
25 Tom Thumb, I'm yours, if you with me will go.
GLUMDALCA. Oh! stay, Tom Thumb, and you alone shall fill
That bed where twenty giants used to lie.
TOM THUMB. In the balcony that o'er-hangs the stage,
I've seen a whore two 'prentices° engage;   *apprentices*
30 One half a crown does in his fingers hold,
The other shows a little piece of gold;
She the half guinea wisely does purloin,
And leaves the larger and the baser coin.[1]

(Exeunt[2] all but Glumdalca.)

GLUMDALCA. Left, scorned, and loathed for such a chit[3] as this;
35 ʷʷʷ I feel the storm that's rising in my mind,
Tempests and whirlwinds rise, and roll and roar.
I'm all within a hurricane, as if
ˣˣˣ The world's four winds[4] were pent within my carcass.
ʸʸʸ Confusion, horror, murder, guts and death.

ACT 2, Scene 8

(King, Glumdalca.)

KING. ᶻᶻᶻ Sure never was so sad a king as I,
ᵃᵃᵃᵃ My life is worn as ragged as a coat
A beggar wears; a prince should put it off,
ᵇᵇᵇᵇ To love a captive and a giantess.

---

1 *half a crown* Silver coin worth two and a half shillings; *half guinea* Gold coin
smaller than a half crown, worth about ten shillings; *purloin* Steal; *baser* Inferior.
2 *Exeunt* Exit.
3 *chit* Childish, disrespectful young girl.
4 *world's four winds* I.e., winds from the four corners of the earth.

ᵛᵛᵛ Mr. L——¹ takes occasion in this place to commend the great care of our author to preserve the metre of blank verse, in which Shakespeare, Johnson and Fletcher were so notoriously negligent; and the moderns, in imitation of our author, so laudably observant;

      —————————————Then does
  Your Majesty believe that he can be
  A traitor!   *Earl of Essex.*
Every page of *Sophonisba* gives us instances of this excellence.

ʷʷʷ Love mounts and rolls about my stormy mind.   *Aureng-Zebe.*
  Tempests and whirlwinds through my bosom move.   *Cleom.*

ˣˣˣ With such a furious tempest on his brow,
  As if the world's four winds were pent within
  His blust'ring carcass.   *Anna Bullen.*

ʸʸʸ *Verba tragica.*²

ᶻᶻᶻ This speech hath been terribly mauled by the poets.

ᵃᵃᵃᵃ —————————My life is worn to rags;
  Not worth a Prince's wearing.   *Love Triumph.*

ᵇᵇᵇᵇ Must I beg the pity of my slave?
  Must a King beg! But love's a greater king,
  A tyrant, nay a devil that possesses me.
  He tunes the organ of my voice and speaks,
  Unknown to me, within me.   *Sebastian.*

---

1 *Mr. L——* Mr. L——'s identity is uncertain.
2 *Verba tragica* Latin: language of tragedy.

5   Oh love! Oh love! how great a king art thou!
My tongue's thy trumpet, and thou trumpetest,
Unknown to me, within me. ^{cccc} Oh Glumdalca!
Heaven thee designed a giantess to make,
But an angelic soul was shuffled in.
10   ^{dddd} I am a multitude of walking griefs,
And only on her lips the balm is found,
    ^{eeee} To spread a plaster[1] that might cure them all.
GLUMDALCA. What do I hear?
KING.   What do I see?
15   GLUMDALCA.   Oh!
KING.   Ah!
^{ffff} GLUMDALCA. Ah wretched queen!
KING.   Oh! Wretched king!
^{gggg} GLUMDALCA.   Ah!
20   KING.   Oh!

---

1   *plaster* Medicinal substance, usually spread on a bandage.

cccc When thou wer't formed, Heaven did a man begin;
But a brute soul by Chance was shuffled in. *Aureng-Zebe.*

dddd ————I am a multitude
Of walking griefs. New *Sophonisba.*[1]

eeee I will take thy scorpion blood,
And lay it to my grief till I have ease. *Anna Bullen.*

ffff Our Author, who everywhere shows his great penetration into human
nature, here outdoes himself: where a less judicious poet would have raised a
long scene of whining love. He who understood the passions better, and that
so violent an affection as this must be too big for utterance, chooses rather to
send his characters off in this sullen and doleful manner: in which admirable
conduct he is imitated by the author of the justly celebrated *Eurydice.*[2] Dr.
Young seems to point at this violence of passion;
————————————Passion chokes
Their words, and they're the statues of despair.[3]
And Seneca tells us, *"curae leves loquuntur, ingentes stupent."*[4] The story of
the Egyptian King in Herodotus is too well known to need to be inserted; I
refer the more curious reader to the excellent Montaigne, who hath written
an essay on this subject.[5]

gggg To part is Death————
————'Tis Death to part.
————————————Ah.
————————————Oh. *Don Carlos.*[6]

---

1 *New Sophonisba* This line does not occur in Thomson's play, but in Francis Beaumont and
John Fletcher's *The Maid's Tragedy* (1611).
2 *Eurydice* By David Mallet (1731), in which a stage direction reads: "Eurydice kneels to
Periander, who after looking on her for some time with emotion, breaks away without
speaking."
3 *Passion chokes ... of despair* Lines taken from *Busiris.*
4 *curae ... stupent* Latin: "light cares speak, great ones are speechless"; from Seneca's first-
century CE tragedy, *Phaedra.*
5 *story of the Egyptian King* In Herodotus' *Histories,* the king Psammenitus does not cry to
see his daughter enslaved and his son executed, but the suffering of a friend moves him to
tears; he explains that his own misery is too great to express; *excellent Montaigne* In his
essay "*De la Tristesse*" ("Of Sorrow"), Montaigne retells this story and gives other examples of "that melancholic, dumb, and deaf stupefaction which benumbs all our faculties
when oppressed with accidents greater than we are able to bear."
6 *Don Carlos* By Otway (1676). The lines actually occur in John Gay's *The What D'Ye Call
It* (1715), a farce mocking contemporary theater that seems also to have influenced Fielding's *Tragedy.*

ACT 2, Scene 9

(*Tom Thumb, Huncamunca, Parson.*)

PARSON. Happy's the wooing that's not long adoing;
For if I guess aright, Tom Thumb this night
Shall give a being to a new Tom Thumb.
TOM THUMB. It shall be my endeavour so to do.
5   HUNCAMUNCA. Oh! fie upon you, sir, you make me blush.
TOM THUMB. It is the virgin's sign, and suits you well:
    ʰʰʰʰ I know not where, nor how, nor what I am,
    ⁱⁱⁱⁱ I'm so transported, I have lost myself.
HUNCAMUNCA. Forbid it, all ye stars, for you're so small
10   That, were you lost, you'd find yourself no more.
So the unhappy seamstress once, they say,
Her needle in a pottle,¹ lost, of hay;
In vain she looked, and looked, and made her moan,
For ah, the needle was forever gone.
15   PARSON. Long may they live, and love, and propagate,
Till the whole land be peopled with Tom Thumbs.
    ʲʲʲʲ So when the Cheshire cheese² a maggot breeds,
Another and another still succeeds.
By thousands, and ten thousands they increase,
20   Till one continued maggot fills the rotten cheese.

---

1   *pottle* Half-gallon container.
2   *Cheshire cheese* Cheese from the English county of Cheshire.

hhhh Nor know I whether.

    What am I, who or where.   *Busiris.*

    I was I know not what, and am I know not how.   *Gloriana.*

iiii To understand sufficiently the beauty of this passage, it will be necessary that we comprehend every man to contain two selves. I shall not attempt to prove this from philosophy which the poets make so plainly evident.

    One runs away from the other;

        Let me demand your Majesty,

        Why fly you from yourself?   *Duke of Guise.*

In a 2d, one self is a guardian to the other;

        Leave me the care of me.   *Conquest of Granada.*

Again,

        Myself am to myself less near.   *Ibid.*

In the same, the first self is proud of the second;

        I myself am proud of me.   *State of Innocence.*

In a 3d, distrustful of him;

        Fain I would tell, but whisper it in mine ear,

        That none besides might hear, nay not myself.   *Earl of Essex.*

In a 4th, honours him;

        I honour Rome,

        But honour too myself.   *Sophonisba.*

In a 5th, at variance with him;

        Leave me not thus at variance with myself.   *Busiris.*

Again, in a 6th:

        I find myself divided from myself.   *Medea.*[1]

        She seemed the sad effigies of herself.   Banks's *Albion Queens.*

        Assist me, Zulema, if thou would'st be

        The friend thou seemest, assist me against me.[2]

From all which it appears, that there are two selves; and therefore Tom Thumb's losing himself is no such solecism[3] as it hath been represented by men, rather ambitious of criticizing than qualified to criticize.

jjjj Mr. F—— imagines this Parson to have been a Welsh[4] one from his simile.

---

1 *Medea* By Charles Johnson (1730).

2 *Assist me ... against me* Lines taken from *The Conquest of Granada.*

3 *solecism* Mistake in grammar or absurdity, or a breach of good manners or social propriety.

4 *Welsh* Cheese was supposedly the favorite food of any Welshman.

ACT 2, Scene 10

(*Noodle, Grizzle and then Huncamunca.*)

NOODLE. [kkkk] Sure nature means to break her solid chain,[1]
Or else unfix the world, and in a rage,
To hurl it from its axle-tree and hinges;
All things are so confused, the King's in love,
5   The Queen is drunk, the Princess married is.
GRIZZLE. Oh! Noodle, hast thou Huncamunca seen?
NOODLE. I've seen a thousand sights this day, where none
Are by the wonderful bitch herself outdone,
The King, the Queen, and all the court are sights.
10   GRIZZLE. [llll] D——n your delay, you trifler, are you drunk, ha?
I will not hear one word but Huncamunca.
NOODLE. By this time she is married to Tom Thumb.
GRIZZLE. [mmmm] My Huncamunca.
NOODLE. Your Huncamunca.
15   Tom Thumb's Huncamunca, every man's Huncamunca.
GRIZZLE. If this be true all womankind are damned.
NOODLE. If it be not, may I be so myself.
GRIZZLE. See where she comes! I'll not believe a word
Against that face, upon whose [nnnn] ample brow,
20   Sits innocence with majesty enthroned.
GRIZZLE. Where has my Huncamunca been? See here
The licence in my hand!
HUNCAMUNCA.   Alas! Tom Thumb.
GRIZZLE. Why dost thou mention him?
25   HUNCAMUNCA.   Ah me! Tom Thumb.
GRIZZLE. What means my lovely Huncamunca?
HUNCAMUNCA.   Hum!
GRIZZLE. Oh! Speak.
HUNCAMUNCA.   Hum!
30   GRIZZLE.   Ha! Your every word is "Hum."
[oooo] You force me still to answer you Tom Thumb.
Tom Thumb, I'm on the rack, I'm in a flame,
[pppp] Tom Thumb, Tom Thumb, Tom Thumb, you love the name;

---

1   *her solid chain* The great chain of being, a common poetic image of natural order.

^{kkkk} Our author hath been plundered here according to custom;
Great nature break thy chain that links together
The fabric of the world and make a chaos
Like that within my soul.   *Love Triumphant.*
————Startle nature, unfix the globe,
And hurl it from its axle-tree and hinges.   *Albion Queens.*
The tott'ring Earth seems sliding off its props.[1]

^{llll} D——n your delay, ye torturers proceed,
I will not hear one word but Almahide.   *Conq. of Granada.*

^{mmmm} Mr. Dryden hath imitated this in *All for Love.*[2]

ⁿⁿⁿⁿ This Miltonic style abounds in the new *Sophonisba.*
————And on her ample brow
Sat majesty.

^{oooo} Your ev'ry answer still so ends in that,
You force me still to answer you Morat.   *Aureng-Zebe.*

^{pppp} Morat, Morat, Morat, you love the name.   *Aureng-Zebe.*

---

1   *The tott'ring … its props* Lines taken from *The Persian Princess.*
2   *Mr. Dryden … All for Love* Scriblerus Secundus has in mind the exchange in Act 4 Scene
    1, where Anthony asks "My Cleopatra?" and Ventidius replies, "Your Cleopatra; / Dolla-
    bella's Cleopatra / Every man's Cleopatra."

So pleasing is that sound, that were you dumb
35 You still would find a voice to cry "Tom Thumb."
HUNCAMUNCA. Oh! Be not hasty to proclaim my doom,
 My ample heart for more than one has room,
 A maid like me, heaven formed at least for two;
 ᑫᑫᑫᑫ I married him, and now I'll marry you.
40 GRIZZLE. Ha! dost thou own thy falsehood to my face?
 Think'st thou that I will share thy husband's place,
 Since to that office one cannot suffice,
 And since you scorn to dine one single dish on,
 Go, get your husband put into commission,[1]
45 Commissioners to discharge (ye gods) it fine is,
 The duty of a husband to your Highness;
 Yet think not long I will my rival bear,
 Or unrevenged the slighted willow[2] wear;
 The gloomy, brooding tempest, now confined
50 Within the hollow caverns of my mind,
 In dreadful whirl shall roll along the coasts,
 Shall thin the land of all the men it boasts,
 ʳʳʳʳ And cram up ev'ry chink of hell with ghosts.
 ˢˢˢˢ So have I seen, in some dark winter's day,
55 A sudden storm rush down the sky's highway,
 Sweep through the streets with terrible ding dong,
 Gush through the spouts, and wash whole crowds along.
 The crowded shops, the thronging vermin screen,[3]
 Together cram the dirty and the clean,
60 And not one shoe-boy in the street is seen.
HUNCAMUNCA. Oh! fatal rashness should his fury slay,
 My hapless bridegroom on his wedding day;
 I, who this morn, of two chose which to wed,
 May go again this night alone to bed;
65 ᵗᵗᵗᵗ So have I seen some wild unsettled fool,
 Who had her choice of this, and that joint-stool;

---

1 *get your ... into commission* I.e., have his duties taken over by a commissioning body.
2 *slighted willow* The willow was a symbol of unrequited love.
3 *thronging vermin screen* A reference to the fact that few people in the eighteenth century bathed; instead they covered lice and dirt with powder and wigs.

⁹⁹⁹⁹ Here is a sentiment for the virtuous Huncamunca (says Mr. D——s) and yet with the leave of this great man, the virtuous Panthea in *Cyrus* hath an heart every whit as ample;

> For two I must confess are Gods to me,
> Which is my Abradatus first, and thee. *Cyrus the Great.*

Nor is the Lady in *Love Triumphant* more reserved, though not so intelligible;

> ——I am so divided,
> That I grieve most for both, and love both most.[1]

ʳʳʳʳ A ridiculous supposition to anyone who considers the great and extensive largeness of Hell, says a commentator: but not so to those who consider the great expansion of immaterial substance. Mr. Banks makes one soul to be so expanded that Heaven could not contain it;

> The Heavens are all too narrow for her soul. . *Virtue Betrayed.*

The Persian Princess hath a passage not unlike the author of this;

> We will send such shoals of murdered slaves,
> Shall glut Hell's empty regions.

This threatens to fill Hell even though it were empty; Lord Grizzle only to fill up the chinks, supposing the rest already full.

ˢˢˢˢ Mr. Addison is generally thought to have had this simile in his eye when he wrote that beautiful one at the end of the third act of his *Cato*.[2]

ᵗᵗᵗᵗ This beautiful simile is founded on a proverb which does honour to the English language;

> Between two stools the breech falls to the ground.

I am not so pleased with any written remains of the ancients as with those little aphorisms which verbal tradition hath delivered down to us under the title of proverbs. It were to be wished that instead of filling their pages with the fabulous theology of the pagans, our modern poets would think it worth their while to enrich their works with the proverbial sayings of their ancestors. Mr. Dryden hath chronicled one in heroic;

> Two ifs scarce make one possibility. *Conquest of Granada.*

(continued)

---

1   *I am ... love both most* The lines actually appear in *Cleomenes*.
2   *the third act of his Cato* The reference is actually to the end of the second act of Addison's play:

> So, where our wide Numidian wastes extend,
> Sudden, th'impetuous hurricanes descend,
> Wheel through the air, in circling eddies play,
> Tear up the sands, and sweep whole plains away.
> The helpless traveller with wild surprise
> Sees the dry desert all around him rise
> And smothered in the dusty whirlwind dies.

To give the preference to either, loath
And fondly coveting to sit on both:
While the two stools her sitting part confound,
70   Between 'em both fall squat upon the ground.

ACT 3, Scene 1. King Arthur's Palace.

(ᵁᵘᵘᵘ *Ghost solus.*)

GHOST. Hail! ye black horrors of midnight's midnoon!
Ye fairies, goblins, bats and screech-owls, hail!
And oh! ye mortal watchmen, whose hoarse throats[1]
Th'immortal ghosts dread croakings counterfeit,°   *imitate*
5   All hail!—Ye dancing phantoms, who by day
Are some condemned to fast, some feast in fire;[2]
Now play in church-yards, skipping o'er the graves,
To the ᵛᵛᵛᵛ loud music of the silent bell,
All hail!

---

1   *hoarse throats* Watchmen would be hoarse from calling out each hour, from sunset
    to sunrise.
2   *some condemned ... fire* One proverbial idea of Hell was of a place of extremes—there
    would be either too much food or none, for example.

My Lord Bacon is of opinion that whatever is known of arts and sciences might be proved to have lurked in the proverbs of Solomon.[1] I am of the same opinion in relation to those abovementioned: at least I am confident that a more perfect system of ethics, as well as economy, might be compiled out of them, than is at present extant, either in the works of the ancient philosophers, or those more valuable, as more voluminous, ones of the modern divines.

uuuu Of all the particulars in which the modern stage falls short of the ancient, there is none so much to be lamented as the great scarcity of ghosts in the latter. Whence this proceeds, I will not presume to determine. Some are of opinion that the moderns are unequal to that sublime language which a ghost ought to speak. One says ludicrously that ghosts are out of fashion; another that they are properer for comedy; forgetting, I suppose, that Aristotle hath told us that a ghost is the soul of tragedy; for so I render the Ψυχή ὁ μ θος τ ς τραγωδ ας, which M. Dacier, amongst others, hath mistaken, I suppose misled by not understanding the *fabula* of the Latins, which signifies a ghost as well as a fable.[2]

————*Te premet nox, fabulæeque manes.*   Hor.[3]

Of all the ghosts that have ever appeared on the stage, a very learned and judicious foreign critic gives the preference to this of our author. These are his words, speaking of this tragedy:

————*Nec quidquam in illâ admirabilius quam phasma quoddam horrendum, quod omnibus aliis spectris, quibuscum scatet anglorum tragœdia, longè (pace D——isii V. Doctiss. dixerim) prætulerim.*[4]

vvvv We have already given instances of this figure.

---

1   *My Lord Bacon*   Scriblerus Secundus learnedly alludes to Book II of *The Advancement of Learning* (1605), where Francis Bacon explains "we may see in those aphorisms which have place amongst divine writings composed by Solomon the King, of whom the Scriptures testify, that his heart was as the sands of the sea, encompassing the world, and all worldly matters; we see, I say, not a few profound and excellent cautions, precepts, positions, extending to much variety of occasions."

2   *Ψυχή ὁ ... τραγωδ ας*   Greek: "plot is the soul of tragedy," with a pun on "μ θος," which also means "fable"; *M. Dacier*   André Dacier (1651–1722), French classical scholar and translator whose version of Aristotle's *Poetics* was published in England in 1705.

3   *Te premet ... manes*   Latin: "The fabled ghosts and night will press upon you." The lines are taken from the first-century BCE *Odes* of Horace.

4   *Nec quidquam ... prætulerim*   Latin: "Nothing is so admirable as a certain dreadful phantasm, which is much preferable (do not be offended, D[ennis]issi, most learned man) to all the other ghosts with which English tragedy overflows."

ACT 3, Scene 2

(*King, and Ghost.*)

KING. What noise is this? What villain dares,
At this dread hour, with feet and voice profane,
Disturb our royal walls?
GHOST.   One who defies
5   Thy empty power to hurt him; ʷʷʷʷ one who dares
Walk in thy bedchamber.
KING.   Presumptuous slave!
Thou diest!
GHOST.   Threaten others with that word,
10   ˣˣˣˣ I am a ghost, and am already dead.
KING. Ye stars! 'tis well; were thy last hour to come,
This moment had been it; ʸʸʸʸ yet by thy shroud[1]
I'll pull thee backward, squeeze thee to a bladder,[2]
'Till thou dost groan thy nothingness away.

(*Ghost retires.*)

15   Thou fliest! 'Tis well.
ᶻᶻᶻᶻ I thought what was the courage of a ghost!
Yet, dare not, on thy life—Why say I that,
Since life thou hast not?—Dare not walk again,
Within these walls, on pain of the Red Sea.[3]
20   For, if henceforth I ever find thee here,
As sure, sure as a gun, I'll have thee laid—
GHOST. Were the Red Sea a sea of Holland's gin,[4]
The liquor (when alive) whose very smell
I did detest, did loathe—yet for the sake
25   Of Thomas Thumb, I would be laid therein.

---

1   *shroud* Sheet in which a corpse is wrapped for burial.
2   *to a bladder* I.e., like an inflated bag.
3   *Red Sea* Sea between Africa and Asia; one of the places where ghosts could suppos-
    edly be successfully imprisoned, or in which they feared drowning.
4   *Holland's gin* Cheap gin made in Holland. It was popular among the laboring classes
    because of its price.

^{wwww} Almanzor reasons in the same manner;
———————————A ghost I'll be,
And from a ghost, you know, no place is free. *Conq. of Granada.*

^{xxxx} The man who writ this wretched pun (says Mr. D.) would have picked your pocket: which he proceeds to show not only bad in itself, but doubly so on so solemn an occasion.[1] And yet in that excellent play of *Liberty Asserted*, we find something very much resembling a pun in the mouth of a mistress, who is parting with the lover she is fond of;

ULAMAR. Oh, mortal woe! one kiss, and then farewell.
IRENE. The gods have given to others to fare well.
O miserably must Irene fare.

Agamemnon, in *The Victim*, is full as facetious on the most solemn occasion, that of sacrificing his daughter;

Yes, Daughter, yes; you will assist the priest;
Yes, you must offer up your——vows for Greece.

^{yyyy} I'll pull thee backwards by thy shroud to light,
Or else, I'll squeeze thee like a bladder, there,
And make thee groan thyself away to air. *Conquest of Granada.*
Snatch me, ye Gods, this moment into nothing. *Cyrus the Great.*

^{zzzz} So, art thou gone? Thou canst no conquest boast,
I thought what was the courage of a ghost. *Conquest of Granada.*
King Arthur seems to be as brave a fellow as Almanzor, who says most heroically,

In spite of Ghosts, I'll on.[2]

---

1 *The man ... an occasion* Dennis once responded to a terrible pun, "the man that will make such an execrable pun as that in my company, would pick my pocket." In *The Dunciad Variorum*, Pope similarly references this anecdote in order to expose ironically Dennis's own use of puns.
2 *In spite ... I'll on* This line is actually spoken by Oedipus in Lee and Dryden's *Oedipus* (1679).

KING. Ha! said you?

GHOST.   Yes, my liege, I said Tom Thumb,
  Whose father's ghost I am—once not unknown
  To mighty Arthur. But, I see, 'tis true,
30 The dearest friend, when dead, we all forget.

KING. 'Tis he, it is the honest Gaffer Thumb.
  Oh, let me press thee in my eager arms,
  Thou best of ghosts! Thou something more than ghost!

GHOST. Would I were something more, that we again
35 Might feel each other in the warm embrace.
  But now I have th' advantage of my king,
  aaaaa For I feel thee, whilst thou dost not feel me.

KING. But say, bbbbb thou dearest air, Oh! say, what dread,
  Important business sends thee back to earth?

40 GHOST. Oh! then prepare to hear—which, but to hear,
  Is full enough to send thy spirit hence.
  Thy subjects up in arms, by Grizzle led,
  Will, ere the rosy fingered morn shall ope°   *open*
  The shutters of the sky, before the gate
45 Of this thy royal palace, swarming spread:
  ccccc So have I seen[1] the bees in clusters swarm,
  So have I seen the stars in frosty nights,
  So have I seen the sand in windy days,
  So have I seen the ghosts on Pluto's shore,[2]
50 So have I seen the flowers in spring arise,
  So have I seen the leaves in autumn fall,
  So have I seen the fruits in summer smile,
  So have I seen the snow in winter frown.

KING. Damn all thou'st seen!—Dost thou, beneath the shape
55 Of Gaffer Thumb, come hither to abuse me,
  With similies to keep me on the rack?
  Hence—or by all the torments of thy hell,
  ddddd I'll run thee through the body, though thou'st none.

---

1 *So have I seen* This exaggerated verbal formula is intended to parody the reliance of
   contemporary tragedies on overwrought and distracting similes.
2 *Pluto's shore* Pluto was the classical god of the underworld. The shore referred to
   is that of the River Styx, across which souls of the dead would be transported into
   Hades.

aaaaa The ghost of Lausaria in *Cyrus* is a plain copy of this, and is therefore worth reading.

> Ah, Cyrus!
> Thou may'st as well grasp water, or fleet air,
> As think of touching my immortal shade. *Cyrus the Great.*

bbbbb Thou better part of heavenly air. *Conquest of Granada.*

ccccc A string of similes (says one) proper to be hung up in the cabinet of a prince.

ddddd This passage hath been understood several different ways by the commentators. For my part, I find it difficult to understand it at all. Mr. Dryden says,

> I have heard something how two bodies meet,
> But how two souls join, I know not.[1]

So that 'till the body of a spirit be better understood, it will be difficult to understand how it is possible to run him through it.

---

1 *I have … I know not* These lines are taken from *King Arthur*.

GHOST. Arthur, beware; I must this moment hence,
60   Not frighted by your voice, but by the cocks;
        Arthur beware, beware, beware, beware!
        Strive to avert thy yet impending fate;
        For if thou'rt killed today
        Tomorrow all thy care will come too late.

ACT 3, Scene 3

(*King solus.*)

KING. Oh stay, and leave me not uncertain thus!
        And whilst thou tellest me what's like my fate,
        Oh, teach me how I may avert it too!
        Curst be the man who first a simile made!
5   Curst, ev'ry bard who writes! So have I seen
        Those whose comparisons are just and true,
        And those who liken things not like at all.
        The devil is happy, that the whole creation
        Can furnish out no simile to his fortune.

ACT 3, SCENE 4

(*King, Queen.*)

QUEEN. What is the cause, my Arthur, that you steal
        Thus silently from Dollalolla's breast?
        Why dost thou leave me in the ᵉᵉᵉᵉᵉ dark alone,
        When well thou knowest I am afraid of spirits?
5   KING. Oh, Dollalolla! Do not blame my love;
        I hoped the fumes of last night's punch had laid
        Thy lovely eyelids fast. But, oh! I find
        There is no power in drams[1] to quiet wives;
        Each morn, as the returning sun, they wake,
10   And shine upon their husbands.
QUEEN.   Think, oh think!
        What a surprise it must be to the sun,

---

1   *drams* Small draughts of liquor or medicine.

eeeee Cydaria is of the same fearful temper with Dollalolla;
I never durst in darkness be alone.   *Ind. Emp.*

Rising, to find the vanished world away.
What less can be the wretched wife's surprise,
15   When, stretching out her arms to fold thee fast,
She folds her useless bolster in her arms.
fffff Think, think on that—Oh! think, think well on that.
I do remember also to have read
ggggg In Dryden's Ovid's *Metamorphosis*,[1]
20   That Jove in form inanimate did lie
With beauteous Danae; and trust me, Love,
hhhhh I feared the bolster might have been a Jove.
KING. Come to my arms, most virtuous of thy sex;
Oh Dollalolla! were all wives like thee,
25   So many husbands never had worn horns.[2]
Should Huncamunca of thy worth partake,
Tom Thumb indeed were blest. Oh fatal name!
For didst thou know one quarter what I know,
Then would'st thou know—Alas! what thou would'st know!
30 QUEEN. What can I gather hence? Why dost thou speak
Like men who carry raree-shows[3] about,
Now you shall see, gentlemen, what you shall see?
O tell me more, or thou hast told too much.

ACT 3, Scene 5

(*King, Queen, Noodle.*)

NOODLE. Long life attend your Majesties serene,
Great Arthur, King, and Dollalolla, Queen!
Lord Grizzle, with a bold, rebellious crowd,
Advances to the palace, threatening loud,
5   Unless the Princess be delivered straight,
And the victorious Thumb, without his pate,°   *head*
They are resolved to batter down the gate.

---

1 *Dryden's Ovid's Metamorphosis* Though Dryden did translate several tales from
Ovid's *Metamorphoses*, he did not translate the one alluded to here, in which Jove
rapes the nymph Danaë in the form of a shower of gold.
2 *horns* The proverbial sign of a cuckold, a man whose wife has been unfaithful.
3 *raree-shows* Peep shows contained in portable boxes, into which customers could
look for a fee.

ᶠᶠᶠᶠ Think well of this, think that, think every way.   *Sophonisba.*

ᵍᵍᵍᵍᵍ These quotations are more usual in the comic than in the tragic writers.

ʰʰʰʰʰ This distress (says Mr. D——) I must allow to be extremely beautiful, and tends to heighten the virtuous character of Dollalolla, who is so exceeding delicate that she is in the highest apprehension from the inanimate embrace of a bolster. An example worthy of imitation from all our writers of tragedy.

ACT 3, Scene 6

(*King, Queen, Huncamunca, Noodle.*)

KING. See where the Princess comes! Where is Tom Thumb?
HUNCAMUNCA.Oh! Sir, about an hour and half ago
    He sallied out to encounter with the foe,
    And swore, unless his fate had him misled,
5   From Grizzle's shoulders to cut off his head,
    And serve't up with your chocolate in bed.
KING. 'Tis well, I find one devil told us both.
    Come Dollalolla, Huncamunca, come,
    Within we'll wait for the victorious Thumb;
10   In peace and safety we secure may stay,
    While to his arm we trust the bloody fray;
    Though men and giants should conspire with gods,
    iiiii He is alone equal to all these odds.
QUEEN. He is, indeed, a jjjjj helmet to us all,
15   While he supports, we need not fear to fall;
    His arm dispatches all things to our wish,
    And serves up every foe's head in a dish.
    Void is the mistress of the house of care,
    While the good cook presents the bill of fare;[1]
20   Whether the cod, that northern king of fish,
    Or duck, or goose, or pig, adorn the dish.
    No fears the number of her guests afford,
    But at her hour she sees the dinner on the board.°   *sideboard*

ACT 3, SCENE 7. A PLAIN.

(*Lord Grizzle, Foodle, and Rebels.*)

GRIZZLE. Thus far our arms with victory are crowned;
    For though we have not fought, yet we have found
    kkkkk No enemy to fight withal.

---

1 *bill of fare* List of dishes to be served; menu.

iiiii *"Credat Judaeus Apelles. Non ego"* [1] (Says Mr. D.) "For, passing over the absurdity of being equal to odds, can we possibly suppose a little insignificant fellow—I say again, a little insignificant fellow, able to vie with a strength which all the Sampsons and Hercules's of antiquity would be unable to encounter." I shall refer this incredulous critic to Mr. Dryden's defence of his Almanzor;[2] and lest that should not satisfy him, I shall quote a few lines from the speech of a much braver fellow than Almanzor, Mr. Johnson's Achilles;

Though human race rise in embattled hosts .
To force her from my arms—Oh! son of Atreus!
By that immortal pow'r, whose deathless spirit
Informs this earth, I will oppose them all. *Victim.*

jjjjj "I have heard of being supported by a staff" (says Mr. D.) "but never of being supported by an helmet." I believe he never heard of sailing with wings, which he may read in no less a poet than Mr. Dryden;

Unless we borrow wings, and sail through air. *Love Triumphant.*[3]
What will he say to a kneeling valley?
———————————I'll stand
Like a safe valley, that low bends the knee
To some aspiring mountain. *Injured Love.*

I am ashamed of so ignorant a carper, who doth not know that an epithet in tragedy is very often no other than an expletive.[4] Do not we read in the new *Sophonisba* of grinding chains, blue plagues, white occasions, and blue serenity? Nay, 'tis not the adjective only, but sometimes half a sentence is put by way of expletive, as, "beauty pointed high with spirit," in the same play—and, "in the lap of blessing, to be most curst," in the *Revenge.*

kkkkk A victory like that of Almanzor.
Almanzor is victorious without fight. *Conq. of Granada.*

---

1   *Credat ... Non ego* Latin: "Apelles the Jew may believe you, but I do not." The passage is taken from Book I of Horace's *Satires* and had proverbial familiarity.
2   *defence of his Almanzor* Dryden responded to the criticism that his hero "performs impossibilities" in the essay "Of Heroique Plays," prefixed to *The Conquest of Granada.*
3   *Unless we ... through air* This line actually appears in *King Arthur.*
4   *carper* Petty critic; *epithet* Descriptive term; *expletive* Meaningless filler word.

FOODLE.   Yet I,
5   Methinks, would willingly avoid this day,
     lllll This first of April, to engage our foes.
GRIZZLE. This day, of all the days of th' year, I'd choose,
     For on this day my grandmother was born.
     Gods! I will make Tom Thumb an April fool;
10   mmmmm Will teach his wit an errand it ne'er knew,
     And send it post to the Elysian shades.
FOODLE. I'm glad to find our army is so stout,
     Nor does it move my wonder less than joy.
GRIZZLE.   nnnnn What friends we have, and how we came so
     strong,
15   I'll softly tell you as we march along.

ACT 3, Scene 8

(*Tom Thumb, Glumdalca cum suis.*)[1]

(*Thunder and Lightning.*)

TOM THUMB. Oh, Noodle! hast thou seen a day like this?
     ooooo The unborn thunder rumbles o'er our heads,
     ppppp As if the gods meant to unhinge the world;
     And heaven and earth in wild confusion hurl;
5   Yet will I boldly tread the tottering ball.
MERLIN. Tom Thumb!
TOM THUMB.   What voice is this I hear?
MERLIN.   Tom Thumb!
TOM THUMB. Again it calls.
10   MERLIN.   Tom Thumb!
GLUMDALCA.   It calls again.
TOM THUMB. Appear, whoe'er thou art, I fear thee not.
MERLIN. Thou hast no cause to fear; I am thy friend,
     Merlin by name, a conjuror by trade,
15   And to my art thou dost thy being owe.

---

1   *cum suis* Latin: with associates.

^{lllll} Well have we chose an happy day for fight,
For every man in course of time has found
Some days are lucky, some unfortunate. *K. Arthur.*

^{mmmmm} We read of such another in Lee;
Teach his rude wit a flight she never made,
And sent her post to the Elysian shade. *Gloriana.*

ⁿⁿⁿⁿⁿ These lines are copied verbatim in *The Indian Emperor.*

^{ooooo} Unborn thunder rolling in a cloud. *Conq. of Gran.*

^{ppppp} Were Heaven and Earth in wild confusion hurled,
Should the rash Gods unhinge the rolling world,
Undaunted, would I tread the tott'ring ball,
Crushed, but unconquered, in the dreadful *Female Warrior.*[1]
Fall.

---

1   *Female Warrior* Charles Hopkins, *Friendship Improved: or, The Female Warrior* (1700).

TOM THUMB. How!

MERLIN. Hear then the mystic getting of Tom Thumb.

^{qqqqq} *His father was a ploughman plain,*
    His mother milked the cow;
20   *And yet the way to get a son,*
    This couple knew not how.
  Until such time the good old man
    To learned Merlin goes,
  And there to him, in great distress,
25   *In secret manner shows;*
  How in his heart he wished to have
    A child, in time to come,
  To be his heir, though it might be
    No bigger than his thumb:
30   *Of which old Merlin was foretold,*
    That he his wish should have;
  And so a son of stature small,
    The charmer to him gave.

Thou'st heard the past, look up and see the future.

35 TOM THUMB. ^{rrrrr} Lost in amazement's gulf, my senses sink;
  See there, Glumdalca, see another ^{sssss} me?

GLUMDALCA. O sight of horror! See, you are devoured
  By the expanded jaws of a red cow.

MERLIN. Let not these sights deter thy noble mind,
40   ^{ttttt} For lo! a sight more glorious courts thy eyes;
  See from afar a theatre arise;
  There, ages yet unborn shall tribute pay
  To the heroic actions of this day:
  Then buskin tragedy[1] at length shall choose
45   Thy name the best supporter of her muse.[2]

TOM THUMB. Enough; let every warlike music sound,
  We fall contented, if we fall renowned.

---

1 *buskin tragedy* Tragedy in the Athenian dramatic tradition.
2 *muse* Figure of inspiration for poetry or art, so called after the nine Muses, classical goddesses who presided over the arts and learning.

^{qqqqq} See *The History of Tom Thumb*, page 2.[1]

^{rrrrr} ———Amazement swallows up my sense,
And in th'impetuous whirl of circling fate
Drinks down my reason.   *Pers. Princess.*

^{sssss} ———I have outfaced myself,
What! am I two? Is there another me?   *K. Arthur.*

^{ttttt} The character of Merlin is wonderful throughout, but most so in this prophetic part. We find several of these prophecies in the tragic authors, who frequently take this opportunity to pay a compliment to their country, and sometimes to their prince. None but our author (who seems to have detested the least appearance of flattery) would have passed by such an opportunity of being a political prophet.

---

1 *History of Tom Thumb* The text given here follows that found in contemporary versions of the Tom Thumb story.

THE TRAGEDY OF TRAGEDIES 87

ACT 3, Scene 9

(*Lord Grizzle, Foodle, Rebels on one side. Tom Thumb,
Glumdalca on the other.*)

FOODLE. At length the enemy advances nigh,
    uuuuu I hear them with my ear, and see them with my eye.
GRIZZLE. Draw all your swords, for liberty we fight,
    vvvvv And liberty the mustard is of life.
5 TOM THUMB. Are you the man whom men famed Grizzle name?
GRIZZLE. wwwww Are you the much more famed Tom Thumb?
TOM THUMB.   The same.
GRIZZLE. Come on, our worth upon ourselves we'll prove,
    For liberty I fight.
10 TOM THUMB.   And I for love.

(*A bloody engagement between the two armies here, drums
beating, trumpets sounding, thunder and lightning. They fight off
and on several times. Some fall. Grizzle and Glumdalca remain.*)

GLUMDALCA. Turn, coward, turn, nor from a woman fly.
GRIZZLE. Away—thou art too ignoble for my arm.
GLUMDALCA. Have at thy heart.
GRIZZLE.   Nay then, I thrust at thine.
15 GLUMDALCA. You push too well, you've run me through the guts,
    And I am dead.
GRIZZLE.   Then there's an end of one.
TOM THUMB. When thou art dead, then there's an end of two,
    xxxxx Villain.
20 GRIZZLE. Tom Thumb!
TOM THUMB. Rebel!
GRIZZLE. Tom Thumb!
TOM THUMB. Hell!
GRIZZLE. Huncamunca!
25 TOM THUMB. Thou hast it there.
GRIZZLE. Too sure I feel it.
TOM THUMB. To hell then, like a rebel as you are,
    And give my service to the rebels there.

^{uuuuu} I saw the villain, Myron, with these eyes I saw him.   *Busiris.*
In both which places it is intimated that it is sometimes possible to see with
other eyes than your own.

^{vvvvv} "This mustard" (says Mr. D.) "is enough to turn one's stomach: I would
be glad to know what idea the author had in his head when he wrote it." This
will be, I believe, best explained by a line of Mr. Dennis;
    And gave him liberty, the salt of life.   *Liberty Asserted.*
The understanding that can digest the one will not rise at the other.

^{wwwww} HANNIBAL. Are you the Chief whom men famed Scipio call?
    SCIPIO. Are you the much more famous Hannibal?   *Hannib.*

^{xxxxx} Dr. Young seems to have copied this engagement in his *Busiris*:
    MYRON. Villain!
    MEMNON. Myron!
    MYRON. Rebel!
    MEMNON. Myron!
    MYRON. Hell!
    MEMNON. Mandane!

GRIZZLE. Triumph not, Thumb, nor think thou shalt enjoy
30   Thy Huncamunca undisturbed, I'll send
      ^{yyyyy} My ghost to fetch her to the other world;
      ^{zzzzz} It shall but bait at heaven, and then return.
      ^{aaaaaa} But, ha! I feel death rumbling in my brains,
      ^{bbbbbb} Some kinder spright knocks softly at my soul,
35   And gently whispers it to haste away:
      I come, I come, most willingly I come.
      ^{ccccc} So, when some city wife, for country air,
      To Hampstead, or to Highgate[1] does repair;
      Her, to make haste, her husband does implore,
40   And cries, "My dear, the coach is at the door."
      With equal wish, desirous to be gone,
      She gets into the coach, and then she cries—"Drive on!"
TOM THUMB. With those last words ^{dddddd} he vomited his soul,
      Which, ^{eeeeee} like whipped cream, the Devil will swallow
          down.
45   Bear off the body, and cut off the head,
      Which I will to the King in triumph lug;
      Rebellion's dead, and now I'll go to breakfast.

ACT 3, SCENE 10

(*King, Queen, Huncamunca, and Courtiers.*)

KING. Open the prisons, set the wretched free,
      And bid our treasurer disburse six pounds
      To pay their debts. Let no-one weep today.
      Come, Dollalolla; ^{fffff} Curse that odious name!
5   It is so long, it asks an hour to speak it.
      By heavens! I'll change it into Doll, or Loll,
      Or any other civil monosyllable
      That will not tire my tongue.—Come, sit thee down.
      Here seated, let us view the dancer's sports;
10   Bid 'em advance. This is the wedding day
      Of Princess Huncamunca and Tom Thumb;

---

1   *Hampstead ... Highgate* Two villages then located just outside of London.

ʸʸʸʸʸ This last speech of my Lord Grizzle hath been of great service to our poets;
———I'll hold it fast
As life, and when life's gone, I'll hold this last;
And if thou tak'st it from me when I'm slain,
I'll send my ghost, and fetch it back again.   *Conquest of Granada.*

ᶻᶻᶻᶻᶻ My soul should with such speed obey,
It should not bait at Heaven to stop its way.[1]
Lee seems to have had this last in his eye;
'Twas not my purpose, Sir, to tarry there,
I would but go to Heaven to take the air.   *Gloriana.*

ᵃᵃᵃᵃᵃᵃ A rising vapour rumbling in my brains.   *Cleomenes.*

ᵇᵇᵇᵇᵇᵇ Some kind sprite knocks softly at my soul,
To tell me fate's at hand.[2]

ᶜᶜᶜᶜᶜ Mr. Dryden seems to have had this simile in his eye when he says,
My soul is packing up, and just on wing.   *Conquest of Granada.*

ᵈᵈᵈᵈᵈᵈ And in a purple vomit poured his soul.   *Cleomenes.*

ᵉᵉᵉᵉᵉ The Devil swallows vulgar souls
Like whipped cream.   *Sebastian.*

ᶠᶠᶠᶠᶠ How I could curse my name of Ptolemy!
It is so long, it asks an hour to write it.
By Heav'n! I'll change it into Jove, or Mars,
Or any other civil monosyllable,
That will not tire my hand.   *Cleomenes.*

---

1 *My soul … stop its way* Lines taken again from *The Conquest of Granada.*
2 *Some kind … at hand* Lines taken from *Don Sebastian.*

Tom Thumb! who wins two victories ggggg today,
And this way marches, bearing Grizzle's head.

(*A dance here.*)

NOODLE. Oh! monstrous, dreadful, terrible, oh! Oh!
15   Deaf be my ears, forever blind my eyes!
Dumb be my tongue! Feet lame! All senses lost!
hhhhhh Howl wolves, grunt bears, hiss snakes, shriek all ye ghosts!
KING. What does the blockhead mean?
NOODLE.   I mean, my liege,
20   iiiiii Only to grace my tale with decent horror;
Whilst from my garret, twice two stories high,
I looked abroad into the streets below;
I saw Tom Thumb attended by the mob,
Twice twenty shoe boys, twice two dozen links,
25   Chairmen and porters, hackney-coachmen,[1] whores;
Aloft he bore the grizzly head of Grizzle;
When of a sudden through the streets there came
A cow, of larger than the usual size,
And in a moment—guess, oh! guess the rest!
30   And in a moment swallowed up Tom Thumb.
KING. Shut up again the prisons, bid my treasurer
Not give three farthings out—hang all the culprits,
Guilty or not—no matter—ravish virgins,
Go bid the schoolmasters whip all their boys;
35   Let lawyers, parsons, and physicians loose
To rob, impose on, and to kill the world.
NOODLE. Her Majesty the Queen is in a swoon.
QUEEN. Not so much in a swoon, but I have still
Strength to reward the messenger of ill news.

(*Kills Noodle.*)

40   NOODLE. Oh! I am slain.
CLEORA. My lover's killed, I will revenge him so.

(*Kills the Queen.*)

---

1   *links* Torch-bearers; boys who carried the links, torches to light people along the streets; *hackney-coachmen* Those who drive hackney coaches, or coaches for hire.

ggggg Here is a visible conjunction of two days in one, by which our author may have either intended an emblem of a wedding; or to insinuate that men in the honeymoon are apt to imagine time shorter than it is. It brings into my mind a passage in the comedy called *The Coffee-House Politician*;[1]

We will celebrate this day at my house tomorrow.

hhhhhh These beautiful phrases are all to be found in one single speech of *King Arthur, or The British Worthy*.[2]

iiiiii I was but teaching him to grace his tale
With decent horror.   *Cleomenes.*

---

1   *The Coffee-House Politician* By Fielding (1730) himself. The ridiculous line was the result of a composing error: "Tomorrow" was supposed to begin the next sentence.
2   *one single speech of King Arthur* Scriblerus Secundus alludes to a speech in Act III, Scene I:
    But straight a rumbling sound, like bellowing winds,
    Rose and grew loud; confused with howls of wolves,
    And grunts of bears, and dreadful hiss of snakes;
    Shrieks more than human …

HUNCAMUNCA. My Mamma killed! vile murderess, beware.

(*Kills Cleora.*)

DOODLE. This for an old grudge, to thy heart.

(*Kills Huncamunca.*)

MUSTACHA.   And this
45   I drive to thine, Oh Doodle! for a new one.

(*Kills Doodle.*)

KING. Ha! Murderess vile, take that!

(*Kills Mustacha.*)

                                        jjjjjj And take thou this.

(*Kills himself, and falls.*)

So when the child whom nurse from danger guards,
Sends Jack for mustard[1] with a pack of cards;
50   Kings, queens and knaves° throw one another   *male servants*
        down,
'Till the whole pack lies scattered and o'erthrown;
So all our pack upon the floor is cast,
And all I boast is—that I fall the last.

(*Dies.*)

FINIS

—1731

---

1   *Sends Jack for mustard* Plays "52 Pickup."

 jjjjjj We may say with Dryden,
> Death did at length so many slain forget,
> And left the tale, and took them by the great.[1]

I know of no tragedy which comes nearer to this charming and bloody catastrophe than *Cleomenes*, where the curtain covers five principal characters dead on the stage. These lines too,

> I ask no questions then, of who killed who?
> The bodies tell the story as they lie.

seem to have belonged more properly to this scene of our author—nor can I help imagining they were originally his. *The Rival Ladies*[2] too seem beholden to this scene;

> We're now a chain of lovers linked in death,
> Julia goes first, Gonsalvo hangs on her,
> And Angelina hangs upon Gonsalvo,
> As I on Angelina.

No scene, I believe, ever received greater honours than this. It was applauded by several encores, a word very unusual in tragedy— and it was very difficult for the actors to escape without a second slaughter. This I take to be a lively assurance of that fierce spirit of liberty which remains among us, and which Mr. Dryden in his *Essay on Dramatic Poetry*[3] hath observed: "Whether custom" (says he) "hath so insinuated itself into our countrymen, or nature hath so formed them to fierceness, I know not, but they will scarcely suffer combats and other objects of horror to be taken from them." And indeed I am for having them encouraged in this martial disposition; nor do I believe our victories over the French have been owing to anything more than to those bloody spectacles daily exhibited in our tragedies, of which the French stage is so entirely clear.[4]

---

1   *Death did … by the great* Lines taken from *The Conquest of Granada*.
2   *The Rival Ladies* By Dryden (1664).
3   *Essay on Dramatic Poetry* Dryden's essay *Of Dramatic Poesy* (1668), a critical symposium in which several characters debate English drama past and present, was influential for its lively defense of the use of rhyme, its comparison of the English and French theater, and its praise of Shakespeare.
4   *nor do I … so entirely clear* French playwrights, following classical tradition, tended to locate violence offstage.

In Context[1]

Sources and Satiric Models

For a tragedy whose dramatic climax features a diminutive hero being swallowed by a cow "of larger than the usual size," *The Tragedy of Tragedies* is surprisingly bookish—and this is part of Fielding's joke. In the three-act play, Tom Thumb is represented as a superlative hero, while in the notes and apparatus the play itself is treated as the epitome of all tragedies. The disparity between low subject and high style is what produces humor and allows Fielding's mock-editor, "H. Scriblerus Secundus," to warn with unwitting prescience that some critics have understood the play as "a burlesque on the loftiest parts of tragedy." The literary contexts of the *Tragedy* collected in this section thus range from popular ballads to learned parodies, and fall roughly into two categories: sources for the story of Tom Thumb and models for Fielding's satiric approach to this story.

from *The Famous History of Tom Thumb* (1750)

The basic source for *The Tragedy of Tragedies* is the old folktale of Tom Thumb, which had been circulating in chapbook and ballad form for over a century before the little hero set foot upon the stage at the Little Haymarket. Scriblerus alludes in his preface to a contemporary edition of *The History of Tom Thumb*, printed by Edward Midwin ter "at the Looking-Glass on London-Bridge," but since no copy of this or any other chapbook imprint from the early eighteenth century seems to have survived, the precise source for Fielding's dramatization of Thumbian adventures is ambiguous. Extant versions of the story typically focus on incidents that exaggerate the contradiction between the hero's small stature and his "Marvellous Acts of Manhood." Tom is

---

1   Unless otherwise noted, the texts for these contextual materials are taken from first or authoritative early editions. The dates given are those of first publication rather than first performance. Spelling and punctuation have been modernized and normalized, and the conventional eighteenth-century use of capitals and italics for emphasis has been limited. Where relevant, modern critical editions have also been cited.

said to excel Sir Lancelot and the other knights of King Arthur's round table "in acts of cavalry," yet he is also tied to a thistle, borne away by a raven, held captive in a mousetrap, mauled by a cat, swallowed by a fish, and dropped into "a close stool pan." The audience of *The Tragedy of Tragedies* would have been familiar with such incidents, and Fielding uses them as a backdrop to the farcical action of his play. The following excerpts, taken from the first part of *The Famous History of Tom Thumb*, contextualize the physical nature of the hero, as well as the Queen's complaint in Act 1, Scene 5 about the prospect of seeing Tom "from a pudding, mount the throne."

In Arthur's court Tom Thumb did live
    A man of mickle might,
Who was the best of the table round,
    And eke a worthy knight.

In stature but an inch in height,
    Or quarter of a span;
How think you that this valiant knight
    Was proved a valiant man.

His father was a plowman plain,
    His mother milked the cow,
And yet the way to get a son
    This couple knew not how,

Until the time the good old man
    To learned Merlin goes,
And there to him in deep distress,
    In secret manner shows,

How in his heart he'd wish to have
    A child in time to come,
To be his heir, though it might be
    No bigger than his thumb.

Of this old Merlin then foretold,
    How he his wish should have;

And to a son of stature small,
    This charmer to him gave.

No blood nor bones in him should be,
    His shape it being such,
That he should hear him speak, but not
    His wandering shadow touch.

But so unseen to overcome,
    Whereat it pleased him well,
Begat and born in half an hour,
    For to fit his father's will.

And in four minutes grew so fast,
    That he became so tall,
As was the plowman's thumb in length,
    And so she did him call

Tom Thumb, the which the Fairy Queen
    Did give him to his name,
Who with her train of goblins grim
    Unto the christening came.

[...]

Whereas about Christmas time,
    His mother a hog had killed,
And Tom would see the pudding[1] made,
    For fear it should be spoiled.

He sat the candle for to light
    Upon the pudding bowl,
Of which there is unto this day,
    A pretty story told.

---

1   *pudding* Blood or black pudding is a kind of sausage made by cooking pork blood with
    oatmeal until it is thick enough to congeal when cooled. It is a traditional breakfast dish
    in England.

For Tom fell in, and could not be
    For some time after found,
For in the blood and batter he
    Was lost and almost drowned.

And she not knowing of the same,
    Directly after that,
Into the pudding stirred her son,
    Instead of mincing fat.

Now this pudding of the largest size,
    Into the kettle thrown,
Made all the rest to jump about,
    As with a whirlwind blown.

But so it tumbled up and down,
    Within the liquor there,
As if the devil had been boiled,
    Such was the mother's fear.

from George Villiers, Second Duke of Buckingham, *The Rehearsal* (1672)

When, in Act 2, Scene 3 of *The Tragedy of Tragedies*, Huncamunca questions whether Tom Thumb might be the son of "the King of Brentford, old or new," Fielding wittily associates his burlesque tragedy with the plot of the play-within-a-play in his most important dramatic predecessor, *The Rehearsal*. Written by the Second Duke of Buckingham, in collaboration with several other wits,[1] and first performed in 1671 when heroic drama was just beginning to thrive on the English stage, *The Rehearsal* satirized the implausible plots and inflated language that characterized the tragedies of Robert Howard, Elkanah Settle, and, especially, John Dryden. Buckingham caricatures Dryden as Bayes, a fatuous tragedian who attends a rehearsal of his new play concerning rival "kings" who compete for the throne of

---

1   The authorship of *The Rehearsal* is ambiguous, but Buckingham's most likely collaborators are Martin Clifford and Thomas Sprat, with contributions from Abraham Cowley and Edmund Waller.

Brentford, a squalid village west of London. The rehearsal is also attended by a pair of critics, Smith and Johnson, who engage in debate with Bayes and offer running commentary on the absurdities of the play-within. A popular play throughout the eighteenth century, *The Rehearsal* established the satiric convention of the rehearsal-within-a-play, later employed by Fielding in a number of theatrical burlesques, including *The Author's Farce* (1730) and *Pasquin* (1736), subtitled "A Dramatic Satire on the Times: Being the Rehearsal of Two Plays." While it is not a rehearsal play, *The Tragedy of Tragedies* does effectively displace the framing commentary of Bayes and his critics from the front of the stage to the foot of the page, where Scriblerus Secundus offers his remarks on the play in progress. In this sense, the annotated *Tragedy* simulates in print the dramatic self-consciousness of *The Rehearsal*, and of scenes such as the following one from Act 2, in which Bayes interrupts his play to discuss the supposed value of misapplied similes.[1]

(*Enter Prince Pretty-man.*)

PRETTY-MAN. How strange a captive am I grown of late!
Shall I accuse my love, or blame my fate?
My love, I cannot; that is too divine:
And against fate, what mortal dares repine?

(*Enter Cloris.*)

But here she comes.
Sure 'tis some blazing comet, is it not?

(*Lies down.*)

BAYES. Blazing comet! Mark that, I gad, very fine.
PRETTY-MAN. But I am so surprised with sleep, I cannot speak the rest.

(*Sleeps.*)

---

1   The text of *The Rehearsal* is taken from the third edition of 1675, which represents Buckingham's latest revision of the play and which refines the satire on extravagant language.

BAYES. Does not that, now, surprise you, to fall asleep just in the nick? His spirits exhale with the heat of his passion, and all that, and swop falls asleep, as you see. Now, here, she must make a *simile*.

SMITH. Where's the necessity of that, Mr. Bayes?

BAYES. Because she's surprised. That's a general rule: you must ever make a simile when you are surprised; 'tis the new way of writing.

CLORIS. As some tall pine, which we on Ætna,[1] find
T'have stood the rage of many a boist'rous wind,
Feeling without, that flames within do play,
Which would consume his root and sap away;
He spreads his worsted arms unto the skies,
Silently grieves, all pale, repines and dies:
So, shrouded up, your bright eye disappears.
Break forth, bright scorching sun, and dry my tears.

(*Exit.*)

JOHNSON. Mr. Bayes, methinks this simile wants a little application too.

BAYES. No, faith, for it alludes to passion, to consuming, to dying, and all that, which you know are the natural effects of an amour. But I'm afraid this scene has made you sad; for, I must confess, when I writ it, I wept myself.

SMITH. No, truly, sir, my spirits are almost exhaled too, and I am likelier to fall asleep.

(*Prince Pretty-man starts up, and says—*)

PRETTY-MAN. It is resolved.

(*Exit.*)

BAYES. That's all.

SMITH. Mr. Bayes, may one be so bold as to ask you a question, now, and you not be angry?

BAYES. O lord, sir, you may ask me anything, what you please. I vow to gad, you do me a great deal of honour. You do not know me, if you say that, sir.

SMITH. Then pray, sir, what is it that this prince here has resolved in his sleep?

---

1   *Ætna* Volcanic mountain on Sicily's eastern coast.

BAYES. Why, I must confess, that question is well enough asked, for one that is not acquainted with this new way of writing. But you must know, sir, that to out-do all my fellow-writers, whereas they keep their *intrigo* secret, till the very last scene before the dance, I now, sir, (do you mark me)—a—

SMITH. Begin the play, and end it, without ever opening the plot at all?

BAYES. I do so, that's the very plain troth on't. Ha, ha, ha, I do, I gad. If they cannot find it out themselves, e'en let 'em alone for Bayes, I warrant you. [...]

from William Wagstaffe, *A Comment Upon the History of Tom Thumb* (1711)

Though Scriblerus Secundus boasts in his preface that he is "more capable of doing justice to our author than any other man," Fielding was not himself the first satirist to give mock-scholarly treatment to the ballad-story of Tom Thumb. In 1711, William Wagstaffe published an ironic *Comment* on the first part of *The History of Tom Thumb*, intended to parody Joseph Addison's recent critical examination of the old ballads of *Chevy Chase* and the *Two Children in the Wood* in *The Spectator* (nos. 70, 74, and 85). Anticipating both Fielding's burlesque exaggeration of the little hero in *Tom Thumb* and his wrapping of *The Tragedy of Tragedies* in quotation and solemn commentary, Wagstaffe offers a series of learned "observations" that explain the supposedly deep lessons of the ballad and illustrate its sublime "beauties." Like Scriblerus, Wagstaffe grounds his analysis in classical scholarship, deferring to authorities and adducing parallel passages from the ancients. In the following excerpts from the *Comment*, Wagstaffe compares the author of the ballad to Virgil and incongruously evaluates *The History of Tom Thumb* according to epic standards. The *Comment* was reprinted and integrated into the apparatus of a composite edition of the ballad in 1729, under the title *Thomas Redivivus: or, A Compleat History of the Life and Marvellous Actions of Tom Thumb*.

It is a surprising thing that in an age so polite as this, in which we have such a number of poets, critics and commentators, some of the best things that are extant in our language should pass unobserved amidst a crowd of inferior productions, and lie so long buried, as it were, among those that profess such a readiness to give life to everything that is valuable. Indeed we have had an enterprising genius[1] of late that has thought fit to disclose the beauties of some pieces to the world, that might have been otherwise indiscernable, and believed to have been trifling and insipid for no other reason but their unpolished homeliness of dress. And if we were to apply our selves, instead of the classics, to the study of ballads and other ingenious composures of that nature, in such periods of our lives when we are arrived to a maturity of judgment, it is impossible to say what improvement might be made to wit in general, and the art of poetry in particular. And certainly our passions are described in them so naturally, in such lively though simple colours, that how far they may fall short of the artfulness and embellishments of the Romans in their way of writing, *yet cannot fail to please all such readers as are not unqualified for the entertainment by their affectation or ignorance.*[2]

It was my good fortune some time ago to have the library of a school boy committed to my charge, where, among other undiscovered valuable authors, I pitched upon *Tom Thumb* and *Tom Hickathrift*, authors indeed more proper to adorn the shelves of Bodley, or the Vatican,[3] than to be confined to the retirement and obscurity of private study. I have perused the first of these with an infinite pleasure, and a more than ordinary application, and have made some observations on it which may not, I hope, prove unacceptable to the public. And however it may have been ridiculed, and looked upon as an entertainment only for children and those of younger years, may be found perhaps a performance not unworthy the perusal of the judicious, and the model superior to either of those incomparable poems of *Chevy Chase* or *The Children in the Wood*. The design was undoubtedly to recommend virtue, and to show that however anyone may labour under the disadvantages of stature or deformity or the

---

1   *enterprising genius* Joseph Addison.
2   *yet cannot fail ... affectation or ignorance* The italicized passage is a direct quotation from *Spectator* no. 70, where Addison offers a "critic" upon *Chevy Chase*. Italicized passages throughout the *Comment* are parodies of Addison.
3   *Bodley, or the Vatican* That is, the Bodleian Library at Oxford and the Vatican Library, two of the oldest and most prestigious libraries in Europe.

meanness of parentage, yet if his mind and actions are above the ordinary level, those very disadvantages that seem to depress him shall add a lustre to his character.

There are a variety of incidents, dispersed through the whole series of this historical poem, that give an agreeable delight and surprise, *and are such as* Virgil *himself would have touched upon, had the like story been told by that divine poet,* viz. his falling into the pudding bowl and others, which show the courage and constancy, the intrepidity and greatness of soul of this little hero, amidst the greatest dangers that could possibly befall him, and which are the unavoidable attendants of human life.

> *Si fractus illabatur orbis,*
> *Impavidum ferient ruinæ.*[1]

The author of this was unquestionably a person of an universal genius, and if we consider that the age he wrote in must be an age of the most profound ignorance, as appears from the second stanza of the first canto, he was a miracle of a man.

I have consulted Monsieur Le Clerk, and my Dr. B—ly[2] concerning the chronology of this author, who both assure me, though neither can settle the matter exactly, that he is the most ancient of our poets, and 'tis very probable he was a druid, who, as Julius Caesar mentions in his *Commentaries*, used to deliver their precepts in poetry and metre. The author of *The Tale of a Tub* believes he was a Pythagorean philosopher, and held the *Metempsychosis*,[3] and others that he had read Ovid's *Metamorphosis*, and was the first person that ever found out the Philosopher's Stone.[4] A certain antiquary of my

---

1   *Si fractus ... ferient ruinæ* Latin: "If the fractured world should fall to pieces, / The ruins would strike him and find him fearless" (Horace, *Odes* 3.3).
2   *Monsieur Le Clerk* Swiss biblical scholar and encyclopaedist Jean Leclerc (1657–1736), who was famous for promoting critical interpretation or exegesis of scripture; *Dr. B—ly* The classical scholar Dr. Richard Bentley (1662–1742), whose misplaced pedantry was also satirized by Fielding in the preface and notes to the *Tragedy*.
3   *The author ... a Tub* Jonathan Swift (1667–1745), whose Grubstreet narrator lists *Tom Thumb* as the first among "several dozens" of works he claims to have annotated and "handled" in scholarly manner; *Metempsychosis* Greek philosophical term referring to the transmigration of the soul, or the ability of an individual to incarnate from one body to another.
4   *Philosopher's Stone* Legendary alchemical substance believed to be capable of turning base metals such as lead into gold.

acquaintance, who is willing to forget everything he should remember, tells me he can scarcely believe him to be genuine, but if he is, he must have lived some time before the Barons Wars,[1] which he proves, as he does the establishment of religion in this nation, upon the credit of an old monument. [...]

I have took a great deal of pains to set these matters of importance in as clear a light as we critics generally do, and shall begin with the first canto, which treats of our hero's birth and parentage and education, with some other circumstances which you'll find are carried on in a manner not very inelegant, *and cannot fail to please those who are not judges of language, or those who notwithstanding they are judges of language, have a genuine and unprejudiced taste of nature.*[2]

> In Arthur's Court Tom Thumb did live;
> A man of mickle might,
> The best of all the table round,
> And eke a doughty knight,
> In stature but an inch in height,
> Or quarter of a span;
> Then think you not this worthy knight
> Was proved a valiant man.

This beginning is agreeable to the best of the Greek and Latin poets; Homer and Virgil give an idea of the whole poem in a few of the first lines, and here our author draws the character of his hero, and shows what you may expect from a person so well qualified for the greatest undertakings.

In the description of him, which is very fine, he insinuates that though perhaps his person may appear despicable and little, yet you'll find him an hero of the most consummate bravery and conduct, and is almost the same account Statius gives of Tydeus:

---

1 *Barons Wars* The First and Second Barons' Wars were civil wars that took place in England between 1215 and 1217, and 1264 and 1267, respectively.
2 *and cannot fail ... taste of nature* Paraphrase of a passage in *Spectator* no. 85, where Addison discusses the *Two Children in the Wood*.

—Totos infusa per artus,
Major in exiguo regnabat corpore virtus.[1]

[...]

The last four lines of this canto, and the beginning of the next, contain the miraculous adventure of the pudding bowl. And, by the by, we may observe that it was the custom of the Christians at that time to make hog puddings instead of minced pies at Christmas; a laudable custom very probably brought up to distinguish 'em more particularly from the Jews.

> Whereas about a Christmas time,
>   His father an hog had killed,
> And Tom to see the pudding made,
>   Fear that it should be spilled;
> He sat, the candle for to light,
>   Upon the pudding bowl,
> Of which there is unto this day,
>   A pretty pastime told:
> For Tom fell in—

Perhaps some may think it below our hero to stoop to such a mean employment as the poet has here enjoined him, of holding the candle, and that it looks too much like a citizen, or a cot, as the women call it. But if we reflect on the obedience due to parents, as our author undoubtedly did, and the necessities those people laboured under, we cannot but admire at his ready compliance with what could by no means be agreeable to the heroical bent of his inclinations, and perceive what a tender regard he had for the welfare of his family, when he took the strictest care imaginable for the preservation of the hog pudding. And what can be more remarkable? What can raise the sentiments of pity and compassion to an higher pitch, than to see an hero fall into such an unforeseen disaster in the honourable execution of his office? *This certainly is conformable to the way of thinking among the ancient poets, and what a good-natured reader cannot but be affected with.* [...]

---

1 *Totos infusa ... corpore virtus* Latin: "—though his body was smaller, greater valor pervaded every part" (Statius' *Thebaid*, book 1).

The next canto is the story of Tom Thumb's being swallowed by a cow, and his deliverance out of her, which is treated of at large by Giordano Bruno,[1] in his *Spaccio de la Bestia Trionfante*; which book, though very scarce, yet a certain gentleman, who has it in his possession, has been so obliging as to let everybody know where to meet with it. After this, you find him carried off by a raven and swallowed by a giant; and 'tis almost the same story as that of Ganymede and the eagle in Ovid:

> Now by a raven of great strength,
>   Away poor Tom was borne.

> *Nec mora: percusso mendacibus aere pennis*
> *Abripit Iliaden.*[2]

[...]

And now, though I am very well satisfied with this performance, yet according to the usual modesty of us authors, I am obliged to tell the world *it will be a great satisfaction to me, knowing my insufficiency*, if I have given but some hints of the beauties of this poem, which are capable of being improved by those of greater learning and abilities. And I am glad to find by a letter I have received from one of the literati in Holland, that the learned Hussius, a great man of our nation, is about the translation of this piece into Latin verse, which he assures me will be done with a great deal of judgment, in case he has enough of that language to furnish out the undertaking. [...]

I hope nobody will be offended at my asserting things so positively, since 'tis the privilege of us commentators, who understand the meaning of an author seventeen hundred years after he has wrote, much better than ever he could be supposed to do himself. And certainly, a critic ought not only to know what his authors thoughts were when he was writing such and such passages, but how those thoughts came

---

1 *Giordano Bruno* Dominican friar, philosopher, mathematician, and astronomer, who published *Spaccio de la Bestia Trionfante* (*The Expulsion of the Triumphant Beast*) in London in 1584. He was later burned at the stake for heresy by the Roman Inquisition in 1600.

2 *Nec mora: ... Abripet Iliaden* Latin: "With no delay, on fictitious eagle's wings, [Jove] flew off with that beloved Trojan boy" (Ovid, *Metamorphoses*, book 10).

into his head, where he was when he wrote, or what he was doing of; whether he wrote in a garden, a garret, or a coach; upon a lady, or a milkmaid; whether at that time he was scratching his elbow, drinking a bottle, or playing at questions and commands. These are material and important circumstances so well known to the *true commentator*, that were Virgil and Horace to revisit the world at this time, they'd be wonderfully surprised to see the minutest of their perfections discovered by the assistances of *modern criticism*. [...]

from John Gay, *The What D'Ye Call It: A Tragi-Comi-Pastoral Farce* (1715)

For all of its learned wit and sophisticated parody, *The Tragedy of Tragedies* is ultimately a tragedy that makes audiences laugh. In fact, it is this temptation to make merry with the play's "bloody catastrophe" that obliges Scriblerus Secundus to dedicate part of his preface to a pedantic discussion of the "very nature of this tragedy." Scriblerus is made to vindicate "The Life and Death of Tom Thumb the Great" through Latin tags and classical scholarship, but Fielding would have found many more immediate precedents for laughable tragedy. The most famous example was the performance of "The Two Kings of Brentford" in *The Rehearsal*. However, Fielding seems also to have drawn upon the play-within-a-play in John Gay's *The What D'Ye Call It*, a travesty that exposes the pomposity and artificiality of heroic assumptions by having rustics debate love and honor in a pastoral setting. In the following excerpt from the preface to the "Tragi-Comi-Pastoral Farce," Gay addresses critical objections to the play and makes a case for a hybrid drama that defies generic expectations.

As I am the first that have introduced this kind of dramatic entertainment upon the stage, I think it absolutely necessary to say something by way of preface, not only to show the nature of it, but to answer some objections that have already been raised against it by the graver sort of wits, and other interested people.

We have often had tragic-comedies upon the English theatre with success, but in that sort of composition the tragedy and comedy are in distinct scenes, and may be easily separated from each other. But the whole art of the *tragic-comi-pastoral farce*[1] lies in interweaving the several kinds of the drama with each other, so that they cannot be distinguished or separated. The objections that are raised against it as a tragedy are as follow.

First, as to the plot, they deny it to be tragical because its catastrophe is a wedding, which hath ever been accounted comical.

Secondly, as to the characters, that those of a justice of peace, a parish clark, and an embryo's ghost, are very improper to the dignity of tragedy, and were never introduced by the ancients.

Thirdly, they say the sentiments are not tragical, because they are those of the lowest country people.

Lastly, they will not allow the moral to be proper for tragedy, because the end of tragedy being to show human life in its distresses, imperfections and infirmities, thereby to soften the mind of man from its natural obduracy and haughtiness, the moral ought to have the same tendency. But this moral, they say, seems entirely calculated to flatter the audience in their vanity and self-conceitedness.

You all have sense enough to find it out.

To the first objection I answer that it is a disputable point, even among the best critics, whether a tragedy may not have a happy catastrophe; that the French authors are of this opinion, appears from most of their modern tragedies.

In answer to the second objection, I cannot affirm that any of the ancients have either a justice of peace, a parish clark, or an embryo ghost in their tragedies. Yet whoever will look into Sophocles, Euripides, or Seneca[2] will find that they greatly affected to introduce nurses in all their pieces, which everyone must grant to be an inferior character to a justice of peace; in imitation of which also, I have introduced a grandmother and an aunt.

---

1   *tragic-comi-pastoral farce* The generic mixture is likely an echo of Polonius's compliment regarding "the best actors in the world, either for tragedy, comedy, history, pastoral, pastoral-comical, historical-pastoral, tragical-historical, tragical-comical-historical-pastoral, scene individable, or poem unlimited" (Shakespeare, *Hamlet* 2.2).
2   *Sophocles, Euripides, or Seneca* Celebrated Greek and Roman tragedians.

To the third objection, which is the meanness of the sentiments, I answer that the sentiments of princes and clowns have not in reality that difference which they seem to have: their thoughts are almost the same, and they only differ as the same thought is attended with a meanness or pomp of diction, or receive a different light from the circumstances each character is conversant in. But these critics have forgot the precept of their master Horace, who tells them,

> *Tragicus plerumque dolet sermon pedestri.*[1]

In answer to the objection against the moral, I have only this to allege: that the moral of this piece is concealed. And morals that are couched so as to exercise the judgments of the audience have not been disapproved by the best critics.[2] And I would have those that object against it as a piece of flattery consider that there is such a figure as the *irony*.

from Jonathan Swift, *Gulliver's Travels* (1726)

Given that its subject matter is the "Life and Death of Tom Thumb the Great," Fielding's burlesque *Tragedy* frequently emphasizes relative size and problems of proportion. Noodle claims that a chairman's leg is "twice as large" as Tom Thumb. The race of vanquished giants are said to "dwarf" the "giants in Guildhall." And Scriblerus Secundus, in an extended note to Act 1, Scene 3, grounds the dramatic excellence of the play in the stature of its characters: "In short, to exceed on either side is equally admirable, and a man of three foot is as wonderful a sight as a man of nine." The most recent elaboration on these themes was Swift's *Gulliver's Travels*, which almost certainly influenced Fielding's conception of a dwarf hero in a world of giants. The experiences of Tom Thumb in King Arthur's court are analogous to those of Gulliver among the Brobdingnagians in Part 2 of Swift's satiric travelogue. Like Gulliver, Tom is disrespected by characters who assume that size is a reflection of the greatness of soul, is occasionally treated as a mere

---

1   *Tragicus plerumque dolet sermon pedestri* Latin: "In tragedy [we often] grieve in ordinary prose" (Horace, *Ars Poetica*). Fielding uses the same Horatian tag in his preface to the *Tragedy*.
2   [Gay's note] See Bossu's chapter of concealed sentences [a reference to René Le Bossu's *Traité du poème épique* (1675)].

spectacle or "sight," and is beloved by women many times his size— one of whom, Glumdalca, borrows her name from Gulliver's nurse, Glumdalclitch. In the following excerpt from the opening chapter of the "Voyage to Brobdingnag," Gulliver has just arrived in a land whose inhabitants are twelve times his size, leading him to reflect on his earlier adventures in Lilliput, where he was twelve times the size of the miniature inhabitants.

I fell into a high road, for so I took it to be, although it served to the inhabitants only as a foot path through a field of barley. Here I walked on for some time, but could see little on either side, it being now near harvest, and the corn rising at least forty foot. I was an hour walking to the end of this field, which was fenced in with a hedge of at least one hundred and twenty foot high, and the trees so lofty that I could make no computation of their altitude. There was a stile to pass from this field into the next: it had four steps, and a stone to cross over when you came to the uppermost. It was impossible for me to climb this stile, because every step was six foot high, and the upper stone above twenty. I was endeavouring to find some gap in the hedge, when I discovered one of the inhabitants in the next field advancing towards the stile, of the same size with him whom I saw in the sea pursuing our boat. He appeared as tall as an ordinary spire-steeple, and took about ten yards at every stride, as near as I could guess. I was struck with the utmost fear and astonishment, and ran to hide myself in the corn, from whence I saw him at the top of the stile, looking back into the next field on the right hand, and heard him call in a voice many degrees louder than a speaking trumpet. But the noise was so high in the air, that at first I certainly thought it was thunder. Whereupon seven monsters like himself came toward him with reaping hooks in their hands, each hook about the largeness of six scythes. These people were not so well clad as the first, whose servants or labourers they seemed to be. For, upon some words he spoke, they went to reap the corn in the field where I lay. I kept from them at as great a distance as I could, but was forced to move with extreme difficulty; for the stalks of corn were sometimes not above a foot distant, so that I could hardly squeeze my body betwixt them. However, I made a shift to go forward till I came to a part of the field where the corn had been laid by the rain and wind. Here it was impossible for me to advance a step; for the stalks were so interwoven that I could not creep through, and the beards of the fallen ears so strong and pointed, that they pierced through my clothes into my flesh. At the same time, I heard the reapers not above an hundred yards behind me.

Being quite dispirited with toil, and wholly overcome by grief and despair, I lay down between two ridges, and heartily wished I might there end my days. I bemoaned my desolate widow, and fatherless children. I lamented my own folly and willfulness in attempting a second voyage against the advice of all my friends and relations. In this terrible agitation of mind I could not forebear thinking of Lilliput, whose inhabitants looked upon me as the greatest prodigy that ever appeared in the world; where I was able to draw an imperial fleet in my hand, and perform those other actions which will be recorded forever in the chronicles of that empire, while posterity shall hardly believe them, although attested by millions. I reflected what a mortification it must prove to me to appear as inconsiderable in this nation, as one single Lilliputian would be among us. But this, I conceived, was to be the least of my misfortunes. For, as human creatures are observed to be more savage and cruel in proportion to their bulk, what could I expect but to be a morsel in the mouth of the first among these enormous barbarians that should happen to seize me? Undoubtedly philosophers are in the right when they tell us that nothing is great or little otherwise than by comparison. It might have pleased fortune to let the Lilliputians find some nation, where the people were as diminutive with respect to them as they were to me. And who knows but that even this prodigious race of mortals might be equally overmatched in some distant part of the world, whereof we have yet no discovery?

from Alexander Pope, *Peri Bathous: or, The Art of Sinking in Poetry* (1728)

In adopting the mock-scholarly persona of H. Scriblerus Secundus in *The Tragedy of Tragedies*, Fielding associates himself and his satiric vision with Swift, Gay, Pope, and the other famous members of the Scriblerus Club, which during its brief existence met weekly in order to satirize "all the false tastes in learning." Fielding's *Tragedy* shares with works like *A Tale of a Tub* (1704–10), *The Beggar's Opera* (1728), and *The Dunciad* (1728-43) an interest in the modern publishing industry, in literary mediocrity and pretentious scholarship, in the relationship between the commercialization of leisure and literature, and in the erasure of distinctions between "popular" and "polite" culture. But it also employs the characteristic Scriblerian technique of seeming to celebrate what it intends to criticize through parodic imitation so adept as to be superficially indistinguishable from the original. Like the best work of the Scriblerians, *The Tragedy of Tragedies* draws audiences in with the farcical entertainment they enjoy, and then satirizes them for their susceptibility—for the very fact of their being drawn in.

Fielding's *Tragedy* thus treats heroic drama in much the same manner that Pope's *Peri Bathous* had treated bad poetry several years earlier. Published under the pseudonym of "Martinus Scriblerus," the tasteless pedant whom the original Scriblerians took as their eponymous hero, *Peri Bathous* compiles and classifies the poetry of poetasters so as to compose an inverted rhetorical *ars*—rules for *how not to write*. Pope has Scriblerus discuss catachresis, hyperbole, periphrasis, and numerous other tropes and figures that are obviously relevant to Fielding's treatment of a heroic idiom that, in straining for the sublime, often achieved only bathos descending to the ordinary with unintentionally ludicrous results.[1] Instead of "transporting" readers to a higher plane, the representative quotations assembled in the following excerpt from Chapter 5 of *Peri Bathous* exemplify, as Scriblerus Primus puts it, "the felicity of falling gracefully." In a similar way, the passages parodied in the *Tragedy* and collected in the footnotes of Scriblerus Secundus illustrate, as it were, "The Art of Sinking in Drama."

---

1   Both Pope and Fielding exploit the semantic ambiguity of the Greek term *bathous*, which might mean either "elevation" or "depth."

Of the true genius for the profound, and by what it is constituted.

And I will venture to lay it down, as the first maxim and cornerstone of this our art, that whoever would excel therein must studiously avoid, detest, and turn his head from all the ideas, ways, and workings of the pestilent foe to wit and destroyer of fine figures, which is known by the name of *common sense.* His business must be to contact the true *goût de travers,*[1] and to acquire a most happy, uncommon, unaccountable way of thinking.

He is to consider himself as a grotesque painter, whose works would be spoiled by an imitation of nature or uniformity of design. He is to mingle bits of the most various or discordant kinds—landscape, history, portraits, animals—and connect them with a great deal of flourishing, by head or tail, as it shall please his imagination and contribute to his principal end, which is to glare by strong oppositions of colours, and surprise by contrariety of images.

Serpentes avibus geminentur, tigribus agni. Hor.[2]

His design ought to be like a labyrinth, out of which nobody can get clear but himself. And since the great art of all poetry is to mix truth with fiction, in order to join the credible with the surprising, our author shall produce the credible by painting nature in her lowest simplicity, and the surprising by contradicting common opinion. In the very manners he will affect the marvellous; he will draw Achilles with the patience of Job; a prince talking like a jack-pudding;[3] a maid of honour selling bargains;[4] a footman speaking like a philosopher; and a fine gentleman like a scholar. Whoever is conversant in modern plays, may make a most noble collection of this kind, and at the same time form a complete body of modern ethics and morality.

Nothing seemed more plain to our great authors, than that the world had long been weary of natural things. How much the contrary are formed to please is evident from the universal applause daily given to the admirable entertainments of harlequins and magicians on our

---

1 *goût de travers* French: wrong-headed taste.
2 *Serpentes ... agni* Latin: "Serpents will lie down with birds, tigers with lambs." A motto from Horace's *Ars Poetica*, frequently applied satirically to mixed genres and entertainments.
3 *jack pudding* Clown, usually employed as an itinerant entertainer's assistant and used to drum up business.
4 *selling bargains* I.e., bargaining for her body as a prostitute.

stage. When an audience behold a coach turned into a wheelbarrow, a conjuror into an old woman, or a man's head where his heels should be,[1] how are they struck with transport and delight? Which can only be imputed to this cause: that each object is changed into that which hath been suggested to them by their own low ideas before.

He ought therefore to render himself master of this happy and *anti-natural* way of thinking to such a degree, as to be able, on the appearance of any object, to furnish his imagination with ideas infinitely below it. And his eyes should be like unto the wrong end of a perspective glass,[2] by which all the objects of nature are lessened.

For example, when a true genius looks upon the sky, he immediately catches the idea of a piece of blue lutestring,[3] or a child's mantle:

> The skies, whose white spreading volumes scarce have room,
> Spun thin, and wove in nature's finest loom,
> The new-born world in their soft lap embraced,
> And all around their starry mantle cast.[4]

If he looks upon a tempest, he shall have an image of a tumbled bed, and describe a succeeding calm in this manner:

> The ocean, joyed to see the tempest fled,
> New lays his waves, and smoothes his ruffled bed.[5]

The triumphs and acclamations of the angels at the creation of the universe, present to his imagination "the rejoicings of the Lord Mayor's Day";[6] and he beholds those glorious beings celebrating their creator

---

1 *a coach turned … heels should be* Standard tricks of contemporary pantomime, of which Harlequin was the hero.
2 *perspective glass* Telescope.
3 *lutestring* Glossy silk fabric, usually used in ribbon.
4 [Pope's note] *Prince Arthur*, p. 41, 42 [Pope cites Richard Blackmore's ten-book epic poem of 1695, *Prince Arthur*. Although Pope satirizes several dozen poets in *Peri Bathous*, the majority of his quotations are drawn from Blackmore.].
5 [Pope's note] In order to do justice to these great poets, our citations are taken from the best, the last, and most correct editions of their work. That which we use of *Prince Arthur* is in duodecimo, 1714. [Pope again cites Blackmore's *Prince Arthur*; he mischievously has Scriblerus cite from the fourth edition of the poem, which was "enlarged" and therefore more bulky and profuse.]
6 *Lord Mayor's Day* Held in late October or early November, a day of popular festivity and fireworks celebrating the procession to Westminster of the Lord Mayor of the City of London to take his oath of office before the Royal Courts of Justice.

by huzzaing, making illuminations, and flinging squibs, crackers, and sky-rockets:

> Glorious illuminations, made on high
> By all the stars and planets of the sky,
> In just degrees, and shining order placed,
> Spectators charmed, and the blessed dwelling graced.
> Through all th'enlightened air swift fireworks flew,
> Which with repeated shouts glad cherubs threw.
> Comets ascended with their sweeping train,
> Then fell in starry showers and glittering rain.
> In air ten thousand meteors blazing hung,
> Which from th'eternal battlements were flung.[1]

If a man who is violently fond of wit, will sacrifice to that passion his friend or his god, would it not be a shame, if he who is smit with the love of the *Bathos*, should not sacrifice to it all other transitory regards? You shall hear a zealous Protestant deacon invoke a saint, and modestly beseech her to do more for us than providence:

> Look down, bless'd saint, with pity then look down,
> Shed on this land thy kinder influence,
> And guide us through the mists of providence,
> In which we stray.—[2]

Neither will he, if a goodly simile come in his way, scruple to affirm himself an eye-witness of things never yet beheld by man, or never yet in existence, as thus:

> Thus have I seen, in Araby the blessed,
> A phoenix couched upon her funeral nest.[3]

---

1 *Glorious illuminations ... were flung* Another passage from Blackmore's *Prince Arthur*.
2 *Look down, bless'd ... which we stray* From Ambrose Philips's "Lament for Queen Mary" (c. 1695).
3 [Pope's note] Anon. [In fact, Pope likely took the passage from his own juvenile epic, *Alcander, Prince of Rhodes*.]

from Alexander Pope, *The Dunciad Variorum* (1729)

Part of the reason that Fielding has Scriblerus Secundus joke in his preface that some critics have claimed that no author "but Mr. P——" could have produced *The Tragedy of Tragedies* is because the apparatus to the play is consciously modeled on the format of Pope's *Dunciad*, which was expanded in 1729 to include, among other pieces, a publisher's advertisement and prolegomena, a "Dissertation of the Poem" by Martinus Scriblerus, and "Notes *Variorum*" by Scriblerus and several other pseudo-scholars. Scriblerus Secundus is made to follow his satiric ancestor in discussing the origins of the *Tragedy*, tracing its bibliography, and offering a "regular examination" of the play in his preface in terms of "the fable, the moral, the characters, the sentiments, and the diction." Moreover, the annotation to the *Tragedy* combines specious commentary and "parallel passages" in the manner of *The Dunciad Variorum* (which organized its notes into "Remarks" and "Imitations"). In the following lines from Book 1 of *The Dunciad Variorum* (ll. 53–82), the Goddess Dullness takes stock of her cultural influence, reflecting upon the effects of generic miscegenation and linguistic extravagance in a way that anticipates Fielding's treatment of these themes in *The Tragedy of Tragedies*. The corresponding footnotes likewise provide a context for Scriblerus Secundus's attempt to "do justice" to the *Tragedy* in his own ironic notes.

Here she beholds the Chaos dark and deep,
Where nameless somethings in their causes sleep,[1]
'Till genial Jacob, or a warm third-day[2]
Call forth each mass, a poem or a play.

---

1 [Pope's note] That is to say, unformed things, which are either made into poems or plays, as the booksellers or the players bid most. These lines allude to the following in Garth's *Dispensary* [1699], Canto 6:

> Within the chamber of the globe they spy
> The beds where sleeping vegetables lie,
> 'Till the glad summons of a genial ray
> Unbinds the glebe, and calls them out to day.

2 *Jacob* Likely Jacob Tonson (1655/6–1736), a leading publisher who specialized in poetry and drama; *third-day* Playwrights were typically paid the profits of the third (and, if successful, the sixth and ninth) night, but not otherwise.

How hints, like spawn, scarce quick in embryo lie,
How new-born nonsense first is taught to cry,
Maggots[1] half-formed, in rhyme exactly meet,
And learn to crawl upon poetic feet.
Here one poor word a hundred clenches[2] makes,[3]
And ductile dullness new meanders takes;[4]
There motley images her fancy strike,
Figures ill-paired, and similes unlike.
She sees a mob of metaphors advance,
Pleased with the madness of the mazy dance:
How tragedy and comedy embrace;
How farce and epic get a jumbled race;
How time himself stands still at her command,[5]
Realms shift their place, and ocean turns to land.
Here gay description Ægypt glads with showers;[6]
Or gives to Zembla fruits, to Barca flowers;

---

1   *Maggots* Pun on the dual meanings of the word as 1) insect larvae and 2) whimsical ideas.

2   *clenches* Another word for puns.

3   [Pope's note] It may not be amiss to give an instance or two of these operations of *Dullness* out of the authors celebrated in the poem. A great critic formerly held these clenches in such abhorrence, that he declared: "He that would pun, would pick a pocket." Yet Mr. Dennis's works afford us notable examples in this kind. "Alexander Pope hath sent abroad into the world as many *Bulls* as his namesake Pope Alexander."—"Let us take the initial and final letters of his surname, *viz.* A. P—E, and they give you the idea of an *ape.*"— "*Pope* comes from the Latin word *Popa*, which signifies a little wart; or from *Poppysma*, because he was continually *popping* out squibs of wit, or rather *Po-pysmata*, or *Po-pisms.*" DENNIS, *Daily Journal* June 11, 1728.

4   [Pope's note] A parody on another in Garth, Cant. 1. "*How ductile matter new meanders takes.*" [Another imitation from *The Dispensary.*]

5   [Pope's note] Allude to the transgressions of the unities, in the plays of such poets. For the miracles wrought upon the time and place, and the mixture of tragedy, comedy, farce, and epic, see *Pluto and Proserpine, Penelope,* &c. as yet extant. [Pope is referencing Lewis Theobald's pantomime, *Harlequin a Sorcerer, with the Loves of Pluto and Proserpine* (1725), and John Mottley and Thomas Cooke's opera, *Penelope* (1728)].

6   [Pope's note] In the lower *Ægypt* rain is of no use, the overflowing of the Nile being sufficient to impregnate the soil. These six verses represent the inconsistencies in the description of poets, who heap together all glittering and gaudy images, though incompatible in one season, or in one scene.—See the *Guardian* No. 40, printed in the Appendix, parag. 6. See also Eusden's whole works (if to be found). It would not have been unpleasant to have given examples of all these species of bad writing from these authors, but that it is already done in our treatise of the *Bathos*. SCRIBL. [Pope ascribes the note to Scriblerus, but Pope himself had written *Guardian* No. 40, which satirized Ambrose Philips and contemporary pastoral writing.]

Glitt'ring with ice here hoary hills are seen,
There painted valleys of eternal green,
On cold December fragrant chaplets blow,
And heavy harvests nod beneath the snow.
All these and more, the cloud-compelling Queen[1]
Beholds through fogs that magnify the scene.
She, tinseled o'er in robes of varying hues,
With self-applause her wild creation views,
Sees momentary monsters rise and fall,
And with her own fool's colours gilds them all.

**from James Ralph, *The Touch-Stone: or, Historical, Critical, Political,
Philosophical, and Theological Essays on the Reigning Diversions of
the Town* (1728)**

> The wide circulation of the Tom Thumb story in chapbook and bal-
> lad format throughout the seventeenth century ensured that, by the
> early eighteenth century, the diminutive hero had become, as Thomas
> Lockwood explains, "a byword of the hopelessly vulgar or literarily
> contemptible." Satires of the period thus frequently allude to *The His-
> tory of Tom Thumb*, treating it as an ironic standard against which to
> evaluate contemporary literature and culture. For example, in the
> following excerpt from *The Touch-Stone*, a tongue-in-cheek survey of
> "the most taking" of contemporary amusements, James Ralph, writ-
> ing under the pseudonym of "A. Primcock," suggests that one way
> to invigorate the opera and to make it more intelligible to London
> audiences would be for impresarios to take native and "traditionary"
> materials, such as *Whittington and his Cat*, *The Dragon of Wantcliff*,
> and *Tom Thumb*, as their topics. This proposal for a literal ballad-opera
> almost certainly provided a hint for Fielding's *Tom Thumb* and the ex-
> panded *Tragedy*, since Ralph collaborated with Fielding and eventually
> acted as his assistant manager at the Little Haymarket Theatre.

To set this affair in a true light, I beg leave to illustrate this essay
with some of our most noted domestic fables, which must please an
English audience, and at the same time make a beautiful appearance

---

1 [Pope's note.] From Homer's epithet of Jupiter, νεφεληγερέτα Ζεύς. [Greek: cloud-
compelling Zeus. The "Queen" in question is Dullness.]

on the stage. They shall be principally borrowed from a subject which can boast an inexhaustible fund of models for theatrical entertainments, particularly operas; *viz.* knight-errantry, which has in all ages produced so many valuable volumes of romances, memoirs, novels and ballads, either written or oral.

A late eminent ingenious author proposed to the then master of the opera stage, *Whittington and his Cat*,[1] and went so far in the design, as to procure a puss or two, who could purr tolerably in time and tune. But the inconveniencies arising from the number of vermin requisite to be destroyed in order to keep up to the truth of the story blasted that project.

Many worthy patriots among us (through the prejudice of their infant education) would dote upon the representation of *Valentine and Orson*. But the scene through every memorable event of that wonderful history being entirely foreign, I cannot approve of its admission; though I must own the H—y–m–t can never hope to show the world two finer bears than they can produce at present, which would be no small addition to a musical drama.

The generality of this nation would likewise imbibe a fondness for the *Seven Champions of Christendom*, even from their nursery; but the Ac—my not being able to furnish so many heroes at a time, we must drop that design. Though I must say, our own St. George's part[2] would equip us with characters and incidents for a very beautiful drama. [...]

'Tis true, I here digress from my original design of only celebrating old English occurrences. For St. George, though our patron saint, was by birth a Cappadocian, and this particular scene of his life was laid in Egypt, whose king's daughter he freed from that terrible monster. But as my mentioning a dragon may excite the curiosity of many connoisseurs to see such a creature fly or tread on the stage, and hear him sing, I think we need not go from home for a fable whose authority is undisputed, and which can furnish out as noble a monster-scene, as if we had gone to China for the story.

---

1 *Whittington and his Cat* Like *Tom Thumb*, this and the following titles were chapbook and ballad standards.
2 *St. George's part* St. George, the patron saint of England, was portrayed in folk legend as a heroic dragon-slayer.

Most of our countrymen, who are deeply read in the old British ballads (which have been so curiously and carefully collected lately by a judicious antiquary, with learned observations and annotations, by which means many remarkable transactions are preserved in those sing-song annals, which history has neglected),[1] will readily imagine that I hint at the noted combat betwixt *Moor* of *Moor-hall* and *The Dragon of Wantcliff*, which for beauty of fable, variety of incidents, a quantity of the marvellous, and a glorious catastrophe, may vie with any story, ancient or modern.

[...]

Robin Hood and Little John cannot fail of charming the British nation, being undoubtedly a domestic matter of fact. But as no singer in Europe can top the part of Little John but Ber—dt,[2] we must suspend that performance till his return, to bless our eyes.

The London 'Prentice would infallibly gain the hearts of the city, besides the valuable incident of a lion-scene; as the *Abbot of Canterbury* would procure the favour of the clergy, and then the whole audience (in imitation of that polite, agreeable custom practiced at Paris) might join the stage, everybody beating time, and singing *Derry down, down, down,* &c.

Tom Thumb would be a beautiful foundation to build a pretty little pastoral on; his length too being adequate to that of a summer's evening, the belles and beaus might arrive time enough from either park, and enjoy the whole of his affair. Nay, it would admit of some very new scenes, as surprising as true: witness the accident of the pudding, which would be something as uncommon as ever appeared on any stage, not excepting even a Dutch Tragedy —*N.B.* Cu—ni[3] in breeches would make a delightful Tom Thumb.

---

1 *which have been ... history has neglected* Ralph is likely referring to *A Collection of Old Ballads*, which was published in three volumes by James Roberts between 1723 and 1725. This alternately scholarly and satiric anthology of "antique songs written Ages ago" (many of which are alluded to by Ralph) was a surprising bestseller.

2 *Ber—dt* Gaetano Berenstadt (1687–1734), Italian alto castrato who performed in London intermittently between 1717 and 1724 and is best remembered for his fruitful association with George Frideric Handel (1685– 1759).

3 *Cu—ni* Francesca Cuzzoni (1700–70), Italian soprano who was among the most famous (and occasionally infamous) operatic performers in London in the 1720s. Along with Berenstadt and other foreign singers, she was satirized in Hogarth's *Masquerades and Operas* (1724) and Gay's *The Beggar's Opera* (1728).

[...]
I know, the severe deep-read critics will object to the simplicity of these subjects, and the lowness of most of the characters, our present operas being generally formed upon plans of the greatest events, and most celebrated parts of history. To this I answer, that we are not obliged to be always tied down to affairs of that vast moment, some stories of an inferior rank allowing as proper entertainments, as just morality, and as tender sentiments, as where we dwell entirely upon the fates of kings and kingdoms. [...]

from Henry Fielding, *Tom Thumb. A Tragedy.... Written by Scriblerus Secundus* (1730)

The most obvious and important "source" for *The Tragedy of Tragedies* was Fielding's own two-act tragedy, *Tom Thumb*, which debuted on 24 April 1730 and ran for an astonishing forty-one nights in its opening season. The play took its rough outline and several of its episodes from the chapbook story of Tom Thumb, magnifying them into matter for tragedy. In this form, *Tom Thumb* represented a neat parody of heroic plays that exploited the easy visual joke of having a "little insignificant fellow" (acted originally by a teenaged "Miss Jones") perform the role of a larger-than-life hero. But Fielding set about to revise the play almost immediately, recognizing its burlesque potential to ridicule broader corruptions in literature and culture. Thus he has Scriblerus Secundus disclaim responsibility for the first *Tom Thumb* in the preface to the *Tragedy*, where he observes with regret that a "surreptitious copy" of the former has been "published by some ill meaning people under my name." In the following excerpt from the preface to the original play, the author (masquerading as Scriblerus?) explains the advantage of tragedies that provoke laughter and responds to the objections of critics, including those who have carped at the final scene in which Grizzle runs through the ghost of Tom Thumb—a circumstance left out of the revised *Tragedy*.

A preface is become almost as necessary to a play, as a prologue: it is a word of advice to the reader, as the other to the spectator. And as the business of a prologue is to commend the play, so that of the preface is to compliment the actors.

[...]

This preface then was writ at the desire of my bookseller, who told me that some elegant critics had made three great objections to this tragedy, which I shall handle without any regard to precedence. And therefore I begin to defend the last scene of my play against the third objection of these *Kriticks*,[1] which is, to the destroying all the characters in it. This I cannot think so unprecedented as these gentlemen would insinuate, having myself known it done in the first act of several plays. Nay, it is common in modern tragedy for the characters to drop, like the citizens in the first scene of *Oedipus*, as soon as they come upon the stage.[2]

Secondly, they object to the killing a ghost. This (say they) far exceeds the rules of probability. Perhaps it may, but I would desire these gentlemen seriously to recollect whether they have not seen in several celebrated plays, such expressions as these, "kill my soul," "stab my very soul," "bleeding soul," "dying soul," *cum multis aliis*,[3] all of which visibly confess that for a soul or ghost to be killed is no impossibility.

As for the first objection which they make, and the last which I answer, *viz.* to the subject, to this I shall only say, that it is in the choice of my subject I have placed my chief merit.

It is with great concern that I have observed several of our (the *Grubstreet*) tragical writers to celebrate in their immortal lines the actions of heroes recorded in historians and poets, such as Homer or Virgil, Livy or Plutarch, the propagation of whose works is so apparently against the interest of our society, when the romances, novels, and histories, *vulgo* called story-books, of our own people, furnish such abundant and proper themes for their pens, such are *Tom Tram*, *Hickathrift*, &c.[4]

---

1 [Fielding's note] Prefatical language. [The intention is presumably to parody pedantic scholarship by employing pseudo-Greek spelling.]

2 *the first scene of Oedipus* Not the Greek tragedy by Sophocles, but Dryden and Lee's 1679 adaptation, *Oedipus*, which opens with the following stage direction: "The curtain rises to a plaintive tune, representing the present condition of Thebes; dead bodies appear at a distance in the streets; some faintly go over the stage, others drop."

3 *cum multis aliis* Latin: with many others. The notes of Scriblerus detail the looseness with which many tragedians employ the word "soul," but Fielding is satirizing, in particular, James Thomson's overuse of the word in *The Tragedy of Sophonisba* (1730).

4 *Tom Tram*, *Hickathrift* More standard chapbook titles, like *Tom Thumb* itself.

And here I congratulate my contemporary writers, for their having enlarged the sphere of tragedy. The ancient tragedy seems to have had only two effects on an audience, *viz.* It either awakened terror and compassion, or composed those and all other uneasy sensations, by lulling the audience in an agreeable slumber. But to provoke the mirth and laughter of the spectators, to join the sock to the buskin,[1] is a praise only due to modern tragedy.

Having spoken thus much of the play, I shall proceed to the performers, amongst whom if any shone brighter than the rest it was Tom Thumb. Indeed, such was the excellence thereof, that no one can believe unless they see its representation, to which I shall refer the curious. Nor can I refrain from observing how well one of the mutes set off his part. So excellent was his performance, that it out-did even my own wishes.[2] I gratefully give him my share of praise, and desire the audience to refer the whole to his beautiful action.

And now I must return my hearty thanks to the music, who, I believe, played to the best of their skill, because it was for their own reputation, and because they are paid for it. So I have thrown little Tom Thumb on the Town, and hope they will be favourable to him. And for an answer to all censures, take these words of Martial:

> *Seria cum possim, quod delectantia malim*
> *Scribere, Tu, Causa es*—[3]

---

1 *join the sock to the buskin* Emblems for tragedy and comedy, respectively. The "buskin" was the thick-soled boot worn by the actors in Greek tragedy, while comedians wore the low shoe or "sock."
2 *outdid even my own wishes* A repeated joke at the expense of Colley Cibber (1671–1757), playwright and co-manager of Drury Lane, who praised Anne Oldfield's performance in *The Provoked Husband* (1728) in the preface to the published version of the play: "she here outdid her usual outdoing."
3 *Seria cum possim … Tu, Causa es* Latin: "If I choose to write what gives delight, even though I could be a serious poet, you are the reason" (Martial, *Epigrams* [1st century CE], book 5).

"Acting Play" to "Reading Play": Performance, Print, Parody

In Act 1, Scene 6 of Fielding's *The Author's Farce* (1730), the dramatic satire to which *Tom Thumb* originally served as an afterpiece, the book-seller Bookweight draws a valuable distinction between what he calls "acting plays" and "reading plays." Acting plays, Bookweight explains, are "entirely supported by the merit of the actor," while reading plays must "support themselves" by way of their substantive "wit and mean-ing." In revising *Tom Thumb* into *The Tragedy of Tragedies* in 1731, Fielding literalized this distinction by replacing a play whose satire was embodied on the stage with a play that exemplified its satire through the printed page. If the knock-about farce and hilariously bloody ca-tastrophe of *Tom Thumb* made it an acting play, one that needed to be seen in performance to be fully appreciated, the apparatus of 139 footnotes (and 195 individual citations) that Fielding added to the published version of the revised *Tragedy* made it decidedly a reading play, one that encouraged careful analysis of the correlation between text, paratext, and intertext.

Fielding's dramatic sources ironically include the very plays he parodies in the inflated language of the *Tragedy* and which H. Scri-blerus Secundus identifies and cites to their disadvantage in the copi-ous notes. The punning title, *The Tragedy of Tragedies*, implies both that the play is the epitome of all tragedies and that it is actually com-posed of other tragedies—specifically, the tragedies in a "heroic" vein popular in the second half of the seventeenth century. The majority of the 42 plays (by 20 authors) cited in the *Tragedy* were out of date and out of repertory, but Fielding burlesques the heroic drama because, as Robert D. Hume puts it, "it is burlesquable." The overwrought heroic idiom of rant and bombast allowed Fielding to explore the efficacy of language as a medium of communication and to test Scriblerus's paradoxical "postulatum": "that the greatest perfection of the language of a tragedy is that it is not to be understood." The material related to heroic drama collected in this section contextualizes Fielding's objects of parody by offering examples of writing that Scriblerus would praise as "being too high or too low for the understanding."

from John Dryden, *The Conquest of Granada by the Spaniards* and "Of Heroic Plays: An Essay" (1672)

Arguably the most influential poet, playwright, and critic of the Restoration, John Dryden was also the most controversial, in part because of the audacity with which he entered into critical dispute and theorized his own poetic and dramatic practice. In *The Conquest of Granada*, performed in two parts in 1670–71, Dryden established the standard thematic pattern and distinctive style of the heroic drama, primarily through the bombastic speeches of his heroes and heroines. Accordingly, the play is Fielding's favorite single source in *The Tragedy of Tragedies*, being quoted eighteen times. The following exchange, from Act 3, Scene 1 of the first part, sets up the archetypal conflict between love and duty: Almanzor, fierce warrior and defender of the Moors against the Spanish, learns that his beloved Almahide is betrothed to Boabdelin, King of the Moors. Almanzor's passionate reaction to this news is full of the strained conceits and lapses in logic characteristic of the language of heroic drama. It is parodied by Tom Thumb in Act 2, Scene 6 of the *Tragedy*.

ALMAHIDE. Our souls are tied by holy vows above.
ALMANZOR. He signed but his, but I will seal my love.
  I love you better, with more zeal than he.
ALMAHIDE. This day—
  I gave my faith to him, he his to me.
ALMANZOR. Good heaven, thy book of fate before me lay,
  But to tear out the journal of this day.
  Or, if the order of the world below
  Will not the gap of one day allow,
  Give me that minute when she made her vow.
  That minute, even the happy from their bliss might give;
  And those who live in grief, a shorter time would live.
  So small a link, if broke, th'eternal chain
  Would, like divided waters, join again.
  It wonnot be; the fugitive is gone,
  Pressed by the crowd of following minutes on:
  That previous moment's out of nature fled,

And in the heap of common rubbish laid,
Of things that once have been, and are decayed.
ALMAHIDE. Your passion, like a fright, suspends my pain.
It meets, o'erpowers, and beats mine back again.
But, as when tides against the current flow,
The native stream runs its course below,
So, though your griefs possess the upper part,
My own have deeper channels in my heart.
ALMANZOR. Forgive that fury which my soul does move,
'Tis the essay of an untaught first love.
Yet rude, unfashioned truth it does express,
'Tis love just peeping in a hasty dress.
Retire, fair creature, to your needful rest,
There's something noble, labouring in my breast.
This raging fire, which through the mass does move,
Shall purge my dross, and shall refine my love.

If theatrical rant was a staple of the heroic drama, it was mainly because Dryden and many of his contemporaries believed it to be ap-
propriate to the extraordinary circumstances in which heroes like
Almanzor often found themselves. How else might a hero express
his thoughts and feelings at the rise and fall of empires, at forbid-
den love, or, as in the following excerpt from Act 4, Scene 3 of the
second part of *The Conquest of Granada*, at chance encounters with
the supernatural? Fielding parodies this scene in Act 3, Scene 2 of the
Tragedy, where the King likewise threatens to squeeze an impertinent
ghost "to a bladder."

ALMANZOR. A hollow wind comes whistling through that door,
And a cold shivering seizes me all o'er.
My teeth, too, chatter with sudden fright:
These are the raptures of too fierce delight!
The combat of the tyrants, Hope and Fear,
Which hearts, for want of field-room, cannot bear.
I grow impatient, this or that's the room,
I'll meet her; now, methinks, I hear her come.

(He goes to the door; the ghost of his mother meets him; he starts back; the ghost stands in the door.)

Well mayst thou make thy boast, whate'er thou art,
Thou art the first e'er made Almanzor start.
My legs—
Shall bear me to thee in their own despite:
I'll rush into the covert of thy night,
And pull thee backward by thy shroud, to light.
Or else I'll squeeze thee, like a bladder, there,
And make thee groan thy self away to air.

(The ghost retires.)

So, thou art gone! Thou canst no conquest boast:
I thought what was the courage of a ghost.—
—The grudging of my ague yet remains;
My blood, like icicles, hangs in my veins,
And does not drop; be master of that door,
We two, will not disturb each other more.
I erred a little, but extremes may join;
That door was hell's, but this is heaven's and mine.

Dryden responded to critics of his overblown tragedy in the essay "Of Heroic Plays," which he prefixed to the published version of *The Conquest of Granada*. In the essay, Dryden historicizes the development of the genre from Sir William Davenant's experiments during the Interregnum to his own attempts to make the heroic play "an imitation, in little, of an heroic poem." Dryden argues, in what would become a classic defense of the genre, for a dramatic representation "that is beyond the common words and actions of human life." He boldly extends this license to the appearance of "spectres and magic," to the performance of "impossibilities" by heroes, and to the use of "unnatural" language—all of which are on display in *The Tragedy of Tragedies*. In the following excerpt from the essay, Dryden describes how and why rhymed couplets in iambic pentameter—what came to be known as "*heroic* couplets"—powerfully distinguish heroic speech from ordinary speech.

Whether heroic verse ought to be admitted into serious plays is not now to be disputed: 'tis already in possession of the stage, and I dare confidently affirm that very few tragedies in this age shall be received without it. All the arguments which are formed against it can amount to no more than this: that it is not so near conversation as prose, and therefore not so natural. But it is very clear to all who understand poetry that serious plays ought not to imitate conversation too nearly. If nothing were to be raised above that level, the foundation of poetry would be destroyed. And if you once admit of a latitude, that thoughts may be exalted and that images and actions may be raised above the life, and described in measure without rhyme, that leads you insensibly from your own principles to mine; you are already so far onward of your way that you have forsaken the imitation of ordinary converse. You are gone beyond it; and, to continue where you are is to lodge in the open field, betwixt two inns. You have lost that which you call natural, and have not acquired the last perfection of art. [...]

from John Dryden, *All for Love: or, The World Well Lost* (1678)

If Tom Thumb is the ironic hero of Fielding's play, John Dryden is the hero of the ironic apparatus and notes, where he is effectively made to stand for the genre of heroic drama. Fielding cites Dryden sixty-nine times in *The Tragedy of Tragedies*, which amounts to more than one third of the total number of citations. For the most part, passages from Dryden are used to illustrate the misuses and abuses of language, while being treated by Scriblerus as representative examples of the upside-down sublime. But in at least one instance, Dryden provides Fielding with material for an episode in his plot. The exchange between the giantess Glumdalca and Huncamunca in Act 2, Scene 7 of the *Tragedy* is consciously modeled on the following "altercative" exchange between Octavia and Cleopatra, romantic rivals for Mark Antony, in Act 3, Scene 1 of *All for Love: or, The World Well Lost*. William Hogarth illustrated the dispute between Glumdalca and Huncamunca, with a tiny Tom looking on, for the frontispiece to the 1731 edition of the *Tragedy* (see page 157).

([*Cleopatra*] *meets Octavia with Ventidius. Octavia bears up to her. Their trains come up on either side.*)

OCTAVIA. I need not ask if you are Cleopatra:
Your haughty carriage—
CLEOPATRA.   —Shows I am a queen.
Nor need I ask who you are.
OCTAVIA.   A Roman:
A name that makes, and can unmake, a queen.
CLEOPATRA. Your lord, the man who serves me, is a Roman.
OCTAVIA. He was a Roman, till he lost that name
To be a slave in Egypt; but I come
To free him thence.
CLEOPATRA.   Peace, peace, my lover's Juno.[1]
When he grew weary of that household clog,
He chose my easier bonds.
OCTAVIA.   I wonder not
Your bonds are easy. You have long been practised
In that lascivious art. He's not the first
For whom you spread your snares: let Caesar witness.
CLEOPATRA. I loved not Caesar; 'twas but gratitude
I paid his love. The worst your malice can
Is but to say the greatest of mankind
Has been my slave. The next, but far above him
In my esteem, is he whom law calls yours,
But whom his love made mine.
OCTAVIA. (*Coming up close to her.*) I would view nearer
That face which has so long usurped my right,
To find th'inevitable charms that catch
Mankind so sure, that ruined my dear lord.
CLEOPATRA. Oh, you do well to search, for had you known
But half these charms, you had not lost his heart.
OCTAVIA. Far be their knowledge from a Roman lady,
Far from a modest wife! Shame of our sex,

---

1 *Juno* As the long-suffering wife (and sister) of Jove, Juno often punished her husband's lovers.

Dost thou not blush to own those black endearments
That make sin pleasing?
CLEOPATRA.   You may blush, who want 'em.
If bounteous nature, if indulgent heav'n
Have giv'n me charms to please the bravest man,
Should I not thank 'em? Should I be ashamed,
And not be proud? I am, that he has loved me;
And when I love not him, heav'n change this face
For one like that.
OCTAVIA.   Thou lov'st him not so well.
CLEOPATRA. I love him better, and deserve him more.
OCTAVIA. You do not—cannot: you have been his ruin.
Who made him cheap at Rome, but Cleopatra?
Who made him scorned abroad, but Cleopatra?
At Actium,[1] who betrayed him? Cleopatra.
Who made his children orphans, and poor me
A wretched widow? Only Cleopatra.
CLEOPATRA. Yet she who loves him best is Cleopatra.
If you have suffered, I have suffered more.
You bear the specious title of a wife
To gild your cause, and draw the pitying world
To favour it; the world contemns poor me,
For I have lost my honour, lost my fame,
And stained the glory of my royal house,
And all to bear the branded name of mistress.
There wants but life, and that too I would lose
For him I love.
OCTAVIA.   Be't so, then; take thy wish.

(*Exit cum suis*.)[2]

---

1 *Actium* Promontory off the west coast of Greece, where, in 31 BCE, Octavian defeated
   Antony and Cleopatra after her fleet of sixty ships sailed prematurely away from the
   sea-battle.
2 *Exit cum suis* I.e., exit with her train of attendants.

from *Thesaurus Dramaticus. Containing all the Celebrated Passages, Soliloquies, Similes, Descriptions, and Other Poetical Beauties in the Body of English Plays, Ancient and Modern, Digested Under Proper Topics,* **2 vols. (1724)**

By the time Fielding staged and published *The Tragedy of Tragedies* in 1731, heroic drama was no longer fashionable. In fact, most of the plays he parodied in the text and which Scriblerus cites in the notes were staged well before he was born, and the vast majority of these had been out of theatrical repertory for many decades. With a few notable exceptions, Fielding's objects of parody were thus conspicuously old-fashioned. Yet if tragedies like *Don Sebastian* (1690), *The Rival Queens* (1677), or *Cyrus the Great* (1696) had largely ceased to be "acting plays," they continued to have currency as "reading plays," thanks to editions of Dryden, Lee, and Banks published in the 1720s, as well as to popular literary handbooks and anthologies that treated excerpted passages from heroic drama as "poetical beauties." These collections could overlook the extravagance of heroic language because they organized representative quotations under thematic "heads" for easy reference, thereby separating theatrical bombast from its dramatic context and celebrating language for its own sake. Take, for instance, the following entry from the *Thesaurus Dramaticus*, which collects under the heading "Sigh" quotations from six of the plays that appear in the notes to the *Tragedy*. While the *Thesaurus Dramaticus* is not likely one of Fielding's direct sources, its contents do suggest what might have motivated his satire.

SIGH

He raised a sigh so hideous and profound,
That it did seem to shatter all his bulk,
And end his being.

Shak. Ham.

Then such deep sighs, heaved from his woeful heart,
As if his sorrowful soul,
Had cracked the strings of life, and burst away!

Lee's Oed.

He knocked his aged breast, and inward groaned,
Like some sad prophet, who foresaw the doom,
Of those whom best he loved, yet could not save.

Dr. Don Seb.

Keep down ye rising sighs,
And murmur in the hollow of my breast;
Run to my heart, and gather more sad wind,
That when the voice of fate shall call you forth,
You may at once rush from the seat of life,
Blow the blood out, and burst me like a bladder!

Lee's Alex.

He fetches sighs,
Which, while he vainly struggles to repress,
With terrible convulsions shake his soul.

Den. Rin. Arm.

His sighs flew from him with so strong a gale,
As if his soul would through his lips exhale.

Lee's Sophon.

A sigh heaves in my breast,
And stops the struggling accents on my tongue!

Rowe's Tam.

Go, my heart's envoy, tender sighs, make haste,
And with your breath swell the soft Zephyrus blast!
Then near that fair one, if you chance to fly,
Tell her in whispers, 'tis for her I die!

Steele's Tender Husb.

I will be calm, press down the rising sighs,
And stifle all the swellings in my heart!

Lee's Caes. Bor.

When my heart was ready with a sigh to cleave in two,
I have with mighty anguish of my soul,
Just at the birth, stifled this still-born sigh,
And forced my heart into a painful smile!

Shak. Troil. Cress.

The murmuring gale revives the drooping flame,
That at thy coldness languished in my breast:
So breathe the gentle Zephyrus on the spring,
And waken every plant and od'rous flower,
Which winter frost had blasted, to new life.

Rowe's Tam.[1]

from James Thomson, *The Tragedy of Sophonisba* (1730)

Most of Fielding's citations are taken from plays that were long out of repertory, and that his audience would likely never have had the opportunity to see acted on the London stage. One exception is James Thomson's *The Tragedy of Sophonisba*, which debuted at Drury Lane on 28 February 1728, and ran for a very respectable eleven nights. The "new" *Sophonisba* was a throwback to the earlier style of heroic rant, and its anachronistic success was an obvious prompt to Fielding's satire in both *Tom Thumb* and *The Tragedy of Tragedies*, which quotes lines from Thomson's play on thirteen occasions. In the following excerpt from Act 3, Scene 2 of *The Tragedy of Sophonisba*, Narva attempts to persuade Masinissa, King of Massylia, out of his love for Sophonisba, the wife of his newly defeated rival Syphax, King of Masæsylia. The scene features several of the speeches parodied by Fielding, including the infamous verbal turn ridiculed in the text and notes to Act 2, Scene 5 of the *Tragedy*: "Oh! Sophonisba! Sophonisba! Oh!"

MASINISSA. Welcome again, my friend,—Come nearer, Narva;
Lend me thine arm, and I will tell thee all,
Unfold my secret heart, whose every pulse
With Sophonisba beats. Nay, hear me out:

---

1   *Rowe's Tam* The shorthand citations in this entry refer to William Shakespeare, *The Tragedy of Hamlet, Prince of Denmark* (performed c. 1601); John Dryden and Nathaniel Lee, *Oedipus* (1679); Dryden, *Don Sebastian, King of Portugal* (1690); Lee, *The Rival Queens: or, The Death of Alexander the Great* (1677); John Dennis, *Rinaldo and Armida* (1699); Lee, *Sophonisba: or, Hannibal's Overthrow* (1676); Nicholas Rowe, *Tamerlane* (1702); Richard Steele, *The Tender Husband* (1705); Lee, *Caesar Borgia: Son of Pope Alexander the Sixth* (1680); Shakespeare, *Troilus and Cressida* (performed c. 1602); and Rowe, *Tamerlane*.

Swift, as I mused, the conflagration spread;
At once too strong, too general, to be quenched.
I love, and I approve it, dote upon her,
Even think these minutes lost I talk with thee.
Heavens! What emotions have possessed my soul!
Snatched by a moment into years of passion.

NARVA. Ah Masinissa!—

MASINISSA.   Argue not against me.
Talk down the circling winds that lift the desert;
And, touched by heaven, when all the forests blaze,
Talk down the flame, but not my stronger love.
I have for love a thousand thousand reasons,
Dear to the heart, and potent o'er the soul.
My ready thoughts all rising, restless all,
Are a perpetual spring of tenderness.
Oh! Sophonisba! Sophonisba! Oh!

NARVA. Is this deceitful day then come to nought?
This day, that set thee on a double throne?
That gave thee Syphax chained, thy deadly foe?
With perfect conquest crowned thee, perfect glory?
Is it so soon eclipsed? And does yon sun,
Yon setting sun, who this fair morning saw thee
Ride through the ranks of long extended war,
As radiant as himself, with every glance
Wheeling the pointed files; and, when the storm
Began, beheld thee tread the rising surge
Of battle high, and drive it on the foe.
Does he now, blushing, see thee sunk so weak?
Caught in a smile? The captive of a look?
I cannot name it without tears.

MASINISSA.   Away!
I'm sick of war, of the destroying trade,
Smoothed o'er, and gilded with the name of glory.
Thou need'st not spread the martial field to me;
My happier eyes are turned another way,
Behold it not; or, if they do, behold it
Shrunk up, far off, a visionary scene,
As to the waking man appears the dream.

NARVA. Or rather as realities appear,
The virtue, pomp, and dignities of life,
In sick disordered dreams.
MASINISSA.   Think not I scorn
The talk of heroes, when oppression rages,
And lawless violence confounds the world.
Who would not bleed with transport for his country,
Tear every dear relation from his heart,
And greatly die to make a people happy,
Ought not to taste of happiness himself,
And is low-souled indeed. But sure, my friend,
There is a time for love, or life were vile!
A sickly circle of revolving days,
Led on by hope, with senseless hurry filled,
And closed by disappointment. Round and round,
Still hope for ever wheels the daily cheat;
Impudent hope! Unjoyous madness all!
Till love comes stealing in, with his kind hours,
His healing lips, his cordial sweets, his cares.
Infusing joy, his joys ineffable!
That make the poor account of life complete,
And justify the gods.
NARVA.   Mistaken Prince,
I blame not love. But—
MASINISSA.   Slander not my passion.
I've suffered thee too far. Take heed, old man.
Love will not bear an accusation, Narva.
NARVA. I'll speak the truth, when truth and friendship call,
Nor fear they frown unkind. Thou has no right
To Sophonisba: she belongs to Rome.[1]
MASINISSA. Ha! She belongs to Rome—'tis true. My thoughts
Where have you wandered, not to think of this?
Think e'er I promised? E'er I loved? Confusion!

---

1 *she belongs to Rome* At this point in the story, Masinissa has defeated Syphax and the
Masæsyli on behalf of his Roman allies, and is under obligation to surrender Sophonisba
so that she can be taken to Rome to appear in a triumphal parade. Masinissa ultimately
convinces the captive princess to drink a cup of poison and commit suicide in order to
avoid degradation and humiliation.

I know not what I say. I should have loved,
Though Jove, in muttering thunder, had forbid it.
But Rome will not refuse so small a boon,
Whose gifts are kingdoms. Rome must grant it sure,
One captive to my wish, one poor request,
So small to them, but oh so dear to me!
Here let my heart confide.
NARVA.   Delusive love!
Through what wild projects is the frantic mind
Beguiled by thee? And think'st thou that the Romans,
The senators of Rome, these gods on earth,
Wise, steady to the right, severely just,
All incorrupt, and like eternal fate
Not to be moved, will listen to the sigh
Of idle love? They, when their country calls,
Who know no pain, no tenderness, no joy,
But bid their children bleed before their eyes;
That they'll regard the light fantastic pangs
Of a fond heart? And with thy kingdom give thee
Their most inveterate foe, from their firm side,
Like Syphax, to delude thee? And the point
Of their own bounty on themselves to turn?
Thou canst not hope it sure. Impossible!
MASINISSA. What shall I do? Be now the friend exerted.
For love and honour press me, love and honour,
All that is dear and excellent in life,
All that or° soothes the man or lifts the hero,   *either*
Bind my soul deep. […]

Reception

It is a measure of the success of *The Tragedy of Tragedies* that Fielding's burlesque is now better known than the majority of the plays he ridiculed. The *Tragedy* was performed over 100 times on the eighteenth-century London stage, and it was widely discussed in contemporary pamphlets, periodicals, and histories of English drama, in correspondence, and in plays featuring characters who reflect on the absurdity of a tragedy that makes audiences laugh. The early reception of the *Tragedy* in many ways contextualizes this success, either by praising Fielding's learning and wit or questioning the prudence of his satire on dead authors and an out-of-date genre. Contemporary commentators examine Fielding's dramatic technique, trace his burlesque predecessors, and debate whether or not *The Tragedy of Tragedies* is a satire on or rather a symptom of declining theatrical taste. In the process, they suggest both the possibilities and problems of burlesque parody, which might easily be mistaken for the thing it ridicules. "You cannot conceive," writes William Shenstone in a 1742 letter to Richard Graves, "how large the number is of those that mistake burlesque for the very foolishness it exposes (which observation I made once at *The Rehearsal*, at *Tom Thumb*, at *Chrononhotonthologos*,[1] all which are pieces of elegant humour)." The miscellaneous material collected in this section explores how Fielding's *Tragedy* was initially promoted and produced, and how it was received by audiences throughout the eighteenth century.

from Advertisements in Contemporary Periodicals (1731)

Like most playwrights of the day, Fielding made extensive use of the periodical press to "puff" his play, and both in the weeks preceding its first performance and during its initial run of twelve nights, *The Tragedy of Tragedies* was advertised in many of London's leading daily and bi-weekly newspapers. Advertisements distinguish between the *Tragedy* and the original *Tom Thumb*, and emphasize the characters

---

1   *Chrononhotonthologos* First performed in 1734 and subtitled "the most tragical tragedy, that ever was tragedized by any company of tragedians," *Chrononhotonthologos* is a burlesque by Henry Carey that shares the satiric vision of Fielding's *Tragedy*.

and devices that lend novelty to the revised play. They also promote the Scriblerus "edition" of the play, which was published on 24 May 1731—the very day of first performance. In fact, the earliest notices of the *Tragedy* give priority to the published version, which suggests that Fielding understood the printed footnotes as an integral part of his new conception of the play.

• from *London Evening Post* (18–20 March 1731)

On Wednesday next will be published, with a curious frontispiece, designed by Mr. Hogarth, and engraved by Mr. Gerard Vandergucht, *The Tragedy of Tragedies: or, The Life and Death of Tom Thumb the Great*. In three acts. As it will be that day acted at the theatre in the Haymarket. With the annotations of Scriblerus Secundus. And at the same time will be published, *The Letter-Writers: or, A New Way to Keep a Wife at Home. A Farce in Three Acts*.[1] As it will be on the same day acted at the theatre in the Haymarket. Written by Scriblerus Secundus. Both printed for J. Roberts[2] in Warwick Lane.

• from *Daily Post* (19 March 1731)

We hear there is now in rehearsal, and will be performed on Wednesday next at the theatre in the Haymarket, *The Tragedy of Tragedies: or, The Life and Death of Tom Thumb the Great*. This tragedy is so far superior to that which already bears the name of *Tom Thumb*, that, omitting the Queen of the Giants, with several other grave personages, together with rivalships, rebellions, battles, similes, &c. not to be found in the first *Tom Thumb*, it is enriched with a ghost, which alone is worth that whole performance. In short, it hath given great satisfaction to the best judges in the closet, and doubtless will do the same on the theatre.

---

1 *The Letter-Writers* This farce, also by Fielding, served as the afterpiece to the *Tragedy* for the first five nights.
2 *J. Roberts* The bookseller of record, James Roberts, was covering for John Watts, who printed both plays.

• from *Daily Post* (22 March 1731)

Never acted before. By the company of comedians at the New Theatre in the Haymarket, on Wednesday next, the 24th day of March, will be presented a new play in three acts, called *The Tragedy of Tragedies: or, The Life and Death of Tom Thumb the Great*. Containing, the rise, marriage, victory, and death of Tom Thumb; the lawful and unlawful loves of King Arthur, Queen Dollallolla; Princess Huncamunca, Queen Glumdalca, Grizzle, &c.; the rivalship, disappointment, and rebellion of Grizzle; the memorable battle between Grizzle and the Queen of the Giants; with the terrible destruction of both armies; and the doleful and tragical apparition of Gaffer Thumb. With several other tragical and historical passages. [...] N.B. Books of the tragedy, with notes by way of key, will be sold at the theatre. [...]

• from *Daily Post* (28 April 1731)

The twelfth day, for the benefit of the author. By the company of comedians at the New Theatre in the Haymarket, this present Wednesday, being the 28th of April, will be presented a new play called *The Tragedy of Tragedies: or, The Life and Death of Tom Thumb the Great*. [...] Note: There being so great a demand for places, pit and boxes will be laid together. No persons to be admitted but by printed tickets, which will be delivered at the office at 5s. Each. [...]

from *The Universal Spectator* (10 April 1731)

Fielding's critics also employed the periodical press, and some of the sharpest attacks on *The Tragedy of Tragedies* appear in contemporary journals. Most of these attacks focus on the seeming ambivalence of Fielding's play and equate the *Tragedy* with the theatrical extravagance it attempts to satirize. In the following excerpt from an issue of *The Universal Spectator*, a correspondent laments the period's "present want of taste," comparing the judicious imitation of nature by Shakespeare and Jonson to the gross corruptions of more recent dramatic entertainments—including heroic tragedies. Yet in citing Fielding's play among these corruptions, "Crito" proves himself to be, like those who fail to understand the meaning of *The Rehearsal*, "utterly insensible of the most poignant strokes of ridicule."

[...] The complaints against the age in which we live are grown so numerous, as to incline some of the best judges to attribute many of them rather to a desire of appearing singular than any real intention of contributing towards an amendment. I should therefore very unwillingly have augmented the number of the querulous had it not been in regard to a case of the utmost importance to the public, in which also I flatter myself I shall advance nothing, but what your readers will admit to be just.

The subject then, both of my complaint and of my letter, shall be our present want of taste, concerning which I shall (with your leave) lay down my sentiments with as much clearness, brevity and candour as I am able. Taste is a metaphorical term, and is taken for our capacity in judging such pieces, as we either read in the closet or behold upon the stage. The signs of a good taste are our giving our approbation to just and fine sentiments, clothed in a corresponding elegancy of expression; as it is a certain evidence of a bad one, our applauding vicious or improper thoughts in any diction whatever.
[...]

Shakespeare and Jonson were the two first writers who gave any lustre to the dramatic performances of our nation; and though we have since them had abundance of authors in that way, yet I believe I shall hardly be contradicted in saying that there have been very few who can with any justice be called their equals, and not so much as one who can be said to have excelled them.

Their distinguishing talent consists in having always kept nature in their view, from whence the propriety of their thoughts recommends them to those who read with judgement; and the entering into the spirit of whatever character they represent moves always the passions of their auditors, according to the excellent observation of Horace:

> —*Si vis me flere, dolendum est*
> *Primum ipsi tibi—*[1]

[...]

---

1   *Si vis me ... Primum ipsi tibi* Latin: "If you wish me to weep, you must first feel grief yourself" (Horace, *Ars Poetica*).

In the works of the dramatic poets who succeeded them, the more exalted characters met with a terrible transformation; their monarchs either thundered in tyrannical bombast or whined forth their amorous complaints with a tenderness below their station. In comedy, the alteration was also for the worse, the grand parts being almost continually a beau or debauchee. In time, the heroes of that set of writers were most of them Almanzors, and the fine gentlemen Dorimants;[1] the one a character altogether out of nature, and the other a disgrace to it.

This naturally leads me to the mention of the source of their errors, which was plainly this: that the poets of those days, either through force or inclination, complied with the prevailing taste of mankind, rather than they would take any pains to amend it. [...] 'Till instead of the manly entertainments of a *Julius* and an *Othello*, the finished workings of a *Volpone* or an *Alchemist*,[2] our stages are polluted with the conjurations of an *Harlequin Faustus*[3] or rendered yet more ridiculous from the feats of *Tom Thumb*.
[...]
Nay, I am sorry to add further that there are some circumstances that almost indicate our being past cure. We are grown utterly insensible of the most poignant strokes of ridicule, and like persons of a ruined constitution, the medicine given to repress the distemper adds but fury to the disease. When that scourge of a declining taste, *The Rehearsal*, is now acted, how many of the spectators do we see gaping at the transactions of the two kings of Brentford, without so much as dreaming that that performance has any other end? Who think Prince Prettyman a real fine gentleman, and the doughty Drawcansir[4] an hero in earnest. In fine, who go away pleas'd with the absurdities of the play, and without the least relish of the finest and most elegant satires.

---

1   *Almanzors, and the fine gentlemen Dorimants* The respective heroes of Dryden's heroic tragedy *The Conquest of Granada* (1672) and George Etherege's comedy of manners *The Man of Mode* (1676).

2   *Julius and an Othello ... Volpone or an Alchemist* Shakespeare's *Julius Caesar* (performed 1599) and *Othello* (performed c. 1604), and Jonson's *Volpone: or, The Fox* (1607) and *The Alchemist* (1612).

3   *Harlequin Faustus* Either *Harlequin Doctor Faustus* or *The Necromancer*, competing pantomimes which were performed in 1723 at Drury Lane and Lincoln's Inn Fields, respectively.

4   *doughty Drawcansir* The ironic hero of *The Rehearsal*, who "frights his mistress, snubs up kings, baffles armies, and does what he will, without regard to good manners, justice, or numbers." Fielding adopted "Alexander Drawcansir" as his editorial pseudonym in *The Covent-Garden Journal* (1752).

Although usually sympathetic to the war on hacks and dunces waged by the Scriblerians, *The Grub-Street Journal* tended to be hostile to Fielding and critical of his audacious pose as a second-generation Scriblerian. For instance, the journal printed the following excerpted poem, an imitation of one of Horace's *Satires* called *The Modern Poets*, in which Fielding is himself represented as a scribbler who condescends (like Colley Cibber) to the low taste of the town and whose popular *Tragedy* inevitably debased traditional literary standards.

That Bays[1] to farce, Sir, turns his tragic strain,
And easy Congreve[2] imitates in vain;
That nonsense oft he writes, then says 'tis new,
Must sure be owned by his admiring few.
For what fond patron can his *Caesar*[3] praise,
His new-year's odes approve, or pastoral lays?[4]
But with his faults, some praises he must share,
When the gay Townly[5] charms the listening fair.
That he's incomparable, yet must we own,
Because he chanced to please the fickle town?
Then fiddling J—[6] might some merit claim,
And Huncamunca rival him in same.
    'Tis not enough, to gain a wild applause,
When crowded theatres espouse your cause.

---

1   *Bays* As it was for Buckingham in *The Rehearsal*, "Bays" is here a satiric epithet for the Poet Laureate, in this case Colley Cibber, who was appointed to the laureateship in 1730 more for his political connections than his poetic talents.
2   *Congreve* William Congreve (1670–1729), celebrated Restoration dramatist.
3   *Caesar* A jibe at Cibber's patchwork tragedy *Caesar in Egypt* (1724), which made extensive use of bombastic language and stage machinery.
4   *new-year's odes* Among his responsibilities as Poet Laureate, Cibber was expected to write odes celebrating the new year; *pastoral lays* Cibber was widely ridiculed for his pastoral farce, *Damon and Phillida* (1729).
5   *gay Townly* In Cibber's *The Provoked Husband* (1728), the lively Lady Townly resists traditional marriage roles, but is eventually reconciled to her husband.
6   *fiddling J——* Samuel Johnson of Cheshire (1691–1773), the dancing-master and dramatist best known for his theatrical extravaganza, *Hurlothrumbo* (1729), in which he sang, danced, and played the fiddle while walking the stage on stilts.

'Tis not enough, to make an audience smile;
But write a strong, correct, yet easy style.
No balmy slumbers should describe a fear,
Nor dull descriptions load the wearied ear.
But aim to soar in Shakespeare's lofty strain,
Or nature draw in Jonson's merry vein.
To F——[1] names unknown, to him have come
The fame of Hickathrift, and brave Tom Thumb:
The brave Tom Thumb does all his thoughts engage:
See, with what noble port, what tragic rage,
His Lilliputian hero treads the stage.

**from William Hatchett and Eliza Haywood, *The Opera of Operas;
or, Tom Thumb the Great. Altered from* The Life and Death of Tom
Thumb the Great. *And Set to Musick after the Italian Manner* (1733)**

Given that *The Tragedy of Tragedies* is built around imitation and exaggeration, it is not surprising that the play lent itself particularly well
to dramatic adaptation. Fielding was inspired by the dramatic works
of Dryden, Banks, Thomson, and others, and subsequent playwrights
were likewise inspired by Fielding's ironic treatment of the language
and conventions of heroic tragedy. Perhaps the most interesting re-
working of Fielding's *Tragedy* is *The Opera of Operas*, a burlesque opera
jointly attributed to William Hatchett and Eliza Haywood, with musical settings composed by John Frederick Lampe. The *Opera* recy-
cles Fielding's plot and retains most of his playtext, adding some new
dialogue and recasting much of the old as musical "airs." Hatchett
and Haywood give Fielding's material an original turn by introduc-
ing, after what appears to be the final scene, two frame characters, Sir
Crit-Operatical and Modely, who discuss the opera's inappropriately
bloody catastrophe and set up a *deus ex machina* which hilariously
revives the dead heroes and heroines of King Arthur's court. Kane
O'Hara drew largely upon *The Opera of Operas* for his popular two-
act burletta, *Tom Thumb* (1780), which superseded Fielding's *Tragedy*
in the final decades of the eighteenth and the early decades of the
nineteenth century.

---

1 F—— Fielding.

(*Enter Sir Crit-Operatical and Modely.*)

MODELY. Well, Sir Crit-Operatical, how like you the entertainment so far?

SIR CRIT-OPERATICAL. Faith, Sir, 'tis as pretty a banquet of dead bodies as a sexton[1] could wish, and variety—but I hope Mr. Modely has a better opinion of the tenderness, as well as regularity, of my musical disposition, than to imagine I can see such a stupid, irregular, bloody, abominable catastrophe, without indignation.

MODELY. Have patience, till you see the catastrophe.[2]

SIR CRIT-OPERATICAL. I would be glad to know who ever saw an Italian opera end tragically? By gad, when we English imitate anything that's foreign, we do it so awkwardly! There's something of whim in the opera, but split me, this will infallibly damn it in the eyes of all good judges. I could almost cudgel the rogue that committed so unparalleled a blunder.

MODELY. But good Sir Crit, keep your temper till you see the catastrophe.

SIR CRIT-OPERATICAL. Catastrophe! Why, the actors are all dead, and unless the author can give them a new being, he will never be able to give his opera another ending.

MODELY. But I hear they are not really dead.

SIR CRIT-OPERATICAL. How! Not dead?

MODELY. No, sir, they are only enchanted. For you must know, Merlin interposed in their fall, and intends, by virtue of the same magic art, to make them all rise again, in order to give a happy conclusion to the opera. And see—he comes.

(*Enter Merlin.*)

---

1   *sexton* Church official responsible for the maintenance of its buildings and management of its graveyard.

2   *catastrophe* In classical tragedy and neoclassical dramatic theory, the catastrophe is the final resolution that brings the various conflicts of the plot to a close.

RECITATIVO.[1]

MERLIN. Sweet goddess of enchanting strains,
   That steal'st, like drink, into men's brains;
   Great trader in soft, melting wane,
   Thou best cradles to our care.
   Lend thy harmonious aid to free
   From magic spell this company.

(*Solemn Music.*)

And first arise, thou fell—thou hideous brute— (*Waves his wand.*)
Thou rav'nous cow!—I do conjure thee to't.

(*A red cow appears.*)
(*Curtain drops.*)

Now, by emetic power, red cannibal. (*Waves his wand.*)
Cast up thy pris'ner, England's Hannibal.[2]
Forth from her growling guts, brave worthy, come,
And be thyself, the Little Great TOM THUMB.

(*He comes out of her mouth, after which she disappears.*)

Now king, now lords, now commons, all arise; (*Waves his wand
   over each as he speaks.*)
Be loose your tongues, and open all your eyes;
Be changed from what ye were, let faction cease,
And ev'ry one enjoy his love in peace.

(*They rise up.*)

---

1   *RECITATIVO* I.e., "recitative," a style of operatic delivery in which a performer adopts the
    rhythms of ordinary speech in song.
2   *Hannibal* Carthaginian general famous for crossing the Alps on elephants to invade Italy
    during the Second Punic War (218–202 BCE).

SIR CRIT-OPERATICAL. Wond'rous, astonishing plot! More sudden than the reprieve in *The Beggar's Opera*[1]—a transformation exceeding all transformation—even the *Comical Transformation*,[2] or any in Ovid's *Metamorphosis*.[3]

RECITATIVO.

KING. O Dollalolla! O my queen!
Thou only art my queen!
QUEEN. O Arthur! O my king!
Thou only art my king!
HUNCAMUNCA. O TOM THUMB!
TOM THUMB. O Huncamunca!
GRIZZLE. Rub well they eyes, O Grizzle, to see clear!
Hast thou been in the moon, or in a sleep?
That matters not, but this I know,
I've slept myself into a better mood.
Pardon my late rebellion, good my liege—
Tom Thumb, be happy in thy Hunky's love—
O sweet Glumdalca! Could'st thou be so with me,
But half a giant, yet an able man.
GLUMDALCA. The offer's kind, and not to be rejected
By one in my sad case—a stranger here—
Some hundred-thousand leagues, or more,
From any of my giant countrymen.

AIR XXXIII.
Dimension, in lovers, takes all knowing lasses,
   From twenty to thirty, or more;

---

1 *the reprieve in The Beggar's Opera* At the close of Gay's play, the condemned hero and highwayman, Macheath, is implausibly reprieved by the Beggar-Poet, on the grounds that "an opera must end happily."
2 *Comical Transformation* An allusion to Thomas Jevon's farce, *The Devil of a Wife: or, A Comical Transformation* (1686), in which the wife of a gentleman and the wife of the cobbler magically change roles.
3 *Ovid's Metamorphosis* Ovid's fifteen-book collection of classical legends features numerous stories of transformation—of gods into animals and humans, and humans into all manner of things.

But little or great, no matter, he passes
  With longing old maids of two score.
For be he short, or be he tall,
  One's better, sure, than none at all.

TOM THUMB. Rebellion's dead, though we are all alive;
  Cured by a miracle, by giving life,
  While others heal by taking it away—
  Enchantment happy! Conjuror most blest!
  Among the faculty of quacks the best.

DUETTE.

TOM THUMB. Tell me, Hunky, without feigning,
  Dost thou longer like abstaining?
HUNCAMUNCA. View my eyes, and know my meaning.
TOM THUMB. I see the lent of love is past;
HUNCAMUNCA. And yet I have not broke my fast;
TOM THUMB. But soon you shall—I'm in the fit.—
HUNCAMUNCA. For what?
TOM THUMB. To love.
HUNCAMUNCA. Then, prithee humour it.
TOM THUMB. Ay, prithee, let us humour it.
HUNCAMUNCA. But dear Tommy, prithee say,
  Wilt thou never go astray?
TOM THUMB. I'll be constant as times go;
  I'll sup abroad a night or so.
HUNCAMUNCA. But if I should do the same?
TOM THUMB. You'd only do like modish dame.
HUNCAMUNCA. Pshaw! Rather let us faithful prove;
  Who shares a lover, does not love.
BOTH. Who shares a lover does not love.
KING. Bravo! Bravissimo!
  Thrice three! Full nine times happy Arthur!
  Show me the king, who is so blessed as I?
  My subjects now no longer by the ears,
  But all shake hands, like friends, with one another.

CHORUS.

Let fierce animosities cease,
Let all married couples agree,
Let each his own wife kiss in peace,
And end all their cavils as we.

FINIS.

from *Observations on the Present Taste for Poetry* (1739)

Unlike many of Fielding's other critics, the anonymous author of *Observations on the Present Taste for Poetry* understands the satiric technique of *The Tragedy of Tragedies*. He chides Fielding, however, for his perceived envy and ill humor in attacking other playwrights in order to establish his own dramatic reputation. Among the playwrights cited in the poem quoted in the *Observations*, only Dryden and Lee come in for real satire in *The Tragedy of Tragedies*. Rowe's *Tamerlane* (1713), Addison's *Cato* (1713), and Fenton's *Mariamne* (1723) are gently alluded to in the notes of Scriblerus Secundus, and Congreve's plays are not mentioned at all.

[...] But what can we say for being pleased with an abuse of all our finest performances together! An attack, at once, on all the great geniuses England has produced for a couple of ages! Whose best endeavours, and some of their greatest beauties, were selected to provoke our contemptuous mirth, by being set in a ridiculous light. And this was done, with wonderful applause, by H—y F—d—g, Esq., *alias*, Scriblerus Secundus. For whom a friend of mine wrote, many years ago, the following lines, *viz.*

Go on, Scriblerus, make our Britons see,
Their country ne'er produced a wit but thee.
Persuade them Fenton scribbled out of rule,
That Addison was mad, and Rowe a fool!
That Congreve's merit was a mere pretence,
That Lee and Dryden wanted common sense!

That fame in their applauses should be dumb,
Your end, no doubt, in writing laboured *Thumb*.
[...]
But now, with honest scorn, the wise regard
The statesman Noodle,[1] and his noodle bard,
Whose baneful morals are a people's jest,
His life a scandal, and his works a pest.
I've shown the bards whose praise you'd take away,
The tribe who 'scape you let me now display!
Shadwell, who once usurped the Laureate's bays,
And D'Urfey, famous long for vulgar plays;
Settle, who fathomed Dullness, thy profound,
And taught heroic fustian high to sound!
Ev'n Dennis scarcely feels the lashing lay![2]
But Dennis is alive[3] and might repay,
Who never patient takes the lash or joke,
But give assailing authors stroke for stroke.
All these were poets dimly doomed to shine,
Whose humble glories have with ease been thine!
What wonder then to them thy satire's blind?
The worst of brutes but seldom hurt their kind.
At length, dull F—d—g, give thy labours o'er,
And show thy spleen, and plague the town no more!
No more to wit by libels make pretence,
But grub thy pen, and show a grain of sense.

---

1   [author's note] A character in *The Tragedy of Tragedies: or, Tom Thumb*.

2   *The tribe who ... the lashing lay* The author catalogues a number of playwrights who had
    previously been satirized for their bad drama, suggesting that they would have been more
    appropriate targets for Fielding: Thomas Shadwell (c. 1642–92), whose brand of "hu-
    mours" comedy was ridiculed by Dryden in *Mac Flecknoe* (1682–84), and who was ironi-
    cally made Poet Laureate when Dryden was deprived of the position in 1688; Thomas
    D'Urfey (1653–1723), whose popular comical farces had given him a reputation as a
    hack and a fool; Elkanah Settle (1648–1724), whose grandiloquent heroic tragedies were
    attacked by Dryden in the second part of *Absalom and Achitophel* (1682) and by Pope in
    The Dunciad (1728); and John Dennis (1657–1734), who is satirized by Fielding more
    for his ill-tempered criticism than for his pretentious drama.

3   [author's note] The authors principally lashed were all dead.

from Giles Jacob, *The Mirrour: or, Satyrical, Panegyrical, Serious, and Humorous on the Present Times* (1733)

If the irony of *The Tragedy of Tragedies* was sometimes lost on London audiences and readers, it is a testament to the success of the play that many of the satires Fielding most admired suffered the same fate. In the following excerpt from the third letter of *The Mirrour*, Giles Jacob groups the *Tragedy* with *The Beggar's Opera* and *The Dunciad* as low works that can only be popular with a tasteless public. He compares these works to *Don Quixote*, expressing regret that the Cervantic vein of "wit and pleasantry" has not taken hold in England. What Jacob overlooks is that, in many ways, *The Tragedy of Tragedies* does for heroic tragedy what *Don Quixote* did for chivalric romance. H. Scriblerus Secundus might himself be seen as a quixotic figure, in that his deep reading in Dryden and Lee, for instance, gives impetus to his battle with scholarly and critical windmills in his notes.

[...] The judgment of the public is, at this time, so much corrupted, that it is become a common saying among some persons when any new poem or play is attended with extraordinary success, that stupid ass, the town, has determined in favour of it, such as *The Dunciad, Tom Thumb, Hurlothrumbo*, &c. Whether this reflection be just or not, will appear on a little examination.

If this great city is thronged with *Tom Thumbs* and *Hurlothrumbos*, 'tis no wonder that they so much applaud their ingenious representatives. Nor is it to be admired, in an age of Don Quixotes, that windmills and dragons[1] are brought upon the polite theatre, and made to usurp the places of men. Indeed, in the gallantry of the Spaniard, there is great wit and pleasantry to alarm the fancy and entertain the mind; but 'tis our misfortune that the English Quixote[2] hardly touches the passions, and has not the least influence on the noble faculties within.

---

1 *Don Quixotes* The eponymous hero of Cervantes's *Don Quixote* (1605, 1615), whose mind is turned by the avid reading of chivalric romances; *windmills and dragons* Both windmills and dragons featured in popular pantomimes of the 1720s.
2 *English Quixote* I.e., the spirit of wit and pleasantry in England; the satiric technique of Cervantes.

Could the famous Shakespeare resume life and visit our present much-frequented theatres, he would not believe that this his native country were in the same situation it was in his days, but would think that Satan had given it a jog towards the land of folly. And when he saw that much greater applause were acquired by a low Newgate opera,[1] than by all his sublime and excellent tragedies, he would certainly pronounce us a nation of fools. And this glorious character is, what I fear, we generally bear amongst the polite foreigners who travel to these kingdoms. [...]

from Samuel Foote, *Taste. A Comedy of Two Acts* (1752)

As Fielding intended it should, the form of *The Tragedy of Tragedies* complicated the meaning of its content, and it took several years for critics fully to appreciate the ingenuity of Fielding's satire. But after the first decade of criticism, the play is routinely treated as a work of wit and a model of dramatic burlesque. In the following excerpt from the dedicatory epistle to his two-act comedy, *Taste*, Samuel Foote justifies his own irregular drama by citing *The Life and Death of Tom Thumb the Great* as an example of what can be achieved by the ironic elevation of the trivial.

[...] It may be thought presumptuous in me to have dignified so short a performance with the name of a comedy; but when my reasons why it cannot be called a farce are considered, the critics must indulge me with the use of that title, at least till they can furnish me with a better. As the follies and absurdities of men are the sole objects of comedy, so the powers of the imagination (plot and incident excepted) are in this kind of writing greatly restrained. No unnatural assemblages, no creatures of the fancy, can procure the protection of the comic muse; men and things must appear as they are. It is employed either in debasing lofty subjects or in raising humble ones.[2] Of the two kinds we have examples in the *Tom Thumb* of Mr. F—, and a travesty of the

---

1 *Newgate opera* I.e., Gay's *The Beggar's Opera*, which ran for 62 consecutive performances in 1728.
2 *debasing lofty subjects or in raising humble ones* Low burlesque (travesty) and high burlesque (mock-heroic), respectively.

Ulysses,[1] where Penelope keeps an alehouse, Telemachus is a tapster, and the hero a recruiting sergeant. In both these instances, you see, nature is reversed [...].

from David Erskine Baker, *Biographia Dramatica: or, A Companion to the Playhouse* (1764)

The entry on *The Tragedy of Tragedies* in Baker's *Biographia Dramatica* represents the first thorough critical explanation of Fielding's play. For all of the confusion over dramatic means and ends that characterizes the play's early reception, Baker provides an accurate history of the *Tragedy*'s development and a sensitive reading of Fielding's burlesque technique. According to Thomas Lockwood, Baker's assessment of the play is "the most knowledgeable and discriminating of the eighteenth century." His observations regarding Fielding's drama in general and *The Tragedy of Tragedies* in particular were quoted by many subsequent critics and set the critical standard for the next hundred years.

THE TRAGEDY OF TRAGEDIES: or, *The Life and Death of Tom Thumb the Great*, 8vo. 1731, with annotations by *Scriblerus Secundus*. This piece first made its appearance in the Little Theatre in the Haymarket, in the year 1730, in one act only;[2] but in the above-mentioned year the success it had met with before, induced the author to enlarge it to the extent of three acts, and bring it on the stage again, first in the Haymarket, and afterwards in Drury Lane Theatre. It is perhaps one of the best burlesques that ever appeared in this or any other language, and may properly be considered as a sequel to the Duke of Buckingham's *Rehearsal*, as it has taken in the absurdities of almost all the writers of tragedy from the period where that piece stops. The scene between Glumdalca and Huncamunca, is a most admirable parody on the celebrated meeting between Octavia and Cleopatra in Dryden's *All for Love*. His love-scenes, his rage, his marriage, his battle, and his bloody catastrophe, are such strong imitations of the tragic rules pursued by the writers of that time, that the satire conveyed cannot escape the observation of any one ever

---

1   *travesty of the Ulysses* An allusion to the ballad opera *Penelope* (1728) by John Mottley and Thomas Cooke.
2   *one act only* Baker is mistaken, since *Tom Thumb* was performed in two acts.

so little conversant with the writers of about half a century past. His similes are beautiful, yet truly ludicrous, and point out strongly the absurdity of a too frequent use of that image in speech. In a word, this piece possesses in the highest degree the principal merit of true burlesque, *viz.* that while it points out the faults of every writer, it leaves no room for the discovery of any in itself. To those who can relish the satire conveyed in it, it is truly delightful, and to those who do not even understand every turn of its humour, it will ever appear at the least agreeable.

from William Hazlitt, "Of the Comic Writers of the Last Century" (1819)

William Hazlitt opens his well-known lecture by asking the provocative question, "why are there comparatively so few good modern comedies?" He answers the question by suggesting that the successes of Wycherley, Congreve, Cibber, Steele, Gay, Fielding, Garrick, Goldsmith, Sheridan, and others have exhausted the comic muse. "Comedy naturally wears itself out," he explains, "and by constantly and successfully exposing the follies and weaknesses of mankind to ridicule, in the end leaves itself nothing worth laughing at." Hazlitt's discussion of Fielding is unique in celebrating the contemporary performance of John Liston in the role of Lord Grizzle, and thereby treating *The Tragedy of Tragedies* as much as an "acting play" as a "reading play."

Fielding was a comic writer, as well as a novelist, but his comedies are very inferior to his novels. They are particularly deficient both in plot and character. The only excellence which they have is that of the style, which is the only thing in which his novels are deficient. The only dramatic pieces of Fielding that retain possession of the stage are, *The Mock Doctor* (a tolerable translation from Molière's *Medecin malgrè lui*),[1] and his *Tom Thumb*, a very admirable piece of burlesque. The absurdities and bathos of some of our celebrated tragic writers could hardly be credited, but for the notes at the bottom of this preposterous medley of bombast, containing his authorities and the parallel

---

1   *Medecin malgrè lui* Fielding's adaptation of Molière's play was first performed at Drury Lane in 1732.

passages. Dryden, Lee, and Shadwell,[1] make no very shining figure there. Mr. Liston[2] makes a better figure in the text. His Lord Grizzle is prodigious. What a name, and what a person! It has been said of this ingenious actor, that "he is very great in Liston"; but he is very even greater in Lord Grizzle. What a wig is that he wears! How flighty, flaunting, and fantastical! Not "like those hanging locks of young Apollo," nor like the serpent-hair of the Furies of Æschylus,[3] but as troublous, though not as tragical as the one, as imposing, though less classical than the other.

"*Que terrible sont ces cheveux gris,*"[4] might be applied to Lord Grizzle's most valiant and magnanimous curls. This sapient courtier's "fell of hair does at dismal treatise rouse and stir as life were in it." His wits seem flying away with the disorder of his flowing locks, and to sit as loosely on our hero's head as the caul of his peruke.[5] What a significant vacancy in his open eyes and mouth! What a listlessness in his limbs! What an abstraction of all thought or purpose! With what an headlong impulse of enthusiasm he throws himself across the stage when he is going to be married, crying "Hey for Doctor's Commons," as if the genius of folly had taken whole-length possession of his person! And then his dancing is equal to the discovery of a sixth sense—which is certainly very different from *common sense*!

---

1 *Shadwell* Shadwell is not actually satirized in the text or notes of *The Tragedy of Tragedies*. Hazlitt might have assumed Fielding would ridicule him because, as the new monarch of "Nonsense" in Dryden's *MacFlecknoe*, Shadwell had become something of a stock dunce.
2 *Mr. Liston* John Liston (c. 1776–1846), one of the leading comic actors of his day. Best known for farcical roles, he established his reputation playing Lord Grizzle at Covent Garden. Hazlitt reviewed a Covent Garden production of *Tom Thumb*, with Liston as Grizzle, for *The Times* (25 September 1817).
3 *Æschylus* Celebrated ancient Greek tragedian (c. 525/24–456/55 BCE).
4 *Que terrible ... gris* French: "How terrible are his gray locks of hair."
5 *His wits seem ... of his peruke* Hazlitt refers to the device of a flying wig, which Liston employed in his role as Lord Grizzle.

"Oh! Heaven, thou art as ugly as the devil." William Hogarth, frontispiece to *The Tragedy of Tragedies: or, The Life and Death of Tom Thumb the Great* (1731). (By permission of the William Andrews Clark Memorial Library, UCLA.)

Hunc. Oh! fay not fmall.

King. This happy News fhall on our Tongue ride Poft,
Our felf will bear the happy News to *Thumb.*
Yet think not, Daughter, that your powerful Charms
Muft ftill detain the Hero from his Arms;
Various his Duty, various his Delight;
Now is his Turn to kifs, and now to fight;
And now to kifs again. So, mighty (*o*) *Jove,*
When with exceffive thund'ring tir'd above,
Comes down to Earth, and takes a Bit — and then,
Flies to his Trade of Thund'ring, back again.

SCENE V.
Grizzle, Huncamunca.

(*p*) *Griz.* Oh! *Huncamunca, Huncamunca,* oh,
Thy pouting Breafts, like Kettle-Drums of Brafs,
Beat everlafting loud Alarms of Joy;
As bright as Brafs they are, and oh, as hard;
Oh *Huncamunca, Huncamunca!* oh!

Hunc. Ha! do'ft thou know me, Princefs as I am,
* That thus of me you dare to make your Game.

(*o*) Juve *with exceffive Thund'ring tir'd above,*
    Comes down for Eafe, *enjoys a Nymph, and then*
    Mounts *dreadful, and to Thund'ring goes again.*

                                        Gloriana.

(*p*) This beautiful Line, which ought, fays Mr. *W——* to be
written in Gold, is imitated in the New *Sophonisba;*
        Oh! *Sophonisba, Sophonisba,* oh!
        Oh! *Narva, Narva,* oh!

The Author of a Song call'd Duke upon Duke, hath improv'd
it.

        Alas! O Nick, *O* Nick, *alas!*

Where, by the help of a little falfe Spelling, you have two
Meanings in the repeated Words.
 * *Edith,* in the *Bloody Brother,* fpeaks to her Lover in the fame
familiar Language.

        Your Grace is full of Game.

                                        Griz.

"Oh! Huncamunca, Huncamunca, oh." Page 26 of *The Tragedy of Tragedies: or, The Life and Death of Tom Thumb the Great* (1731). (By permission of the William Andrews Clark Memorial Library, UCLA.)